Monologues for Young Adults

**60 Original Monologues to
Stand Out, Inspire, and Shine**

Monologues for Young Adults

**60 Original Monologues to
Stand Out, Inspire, and Shine**

Mike Kimmel
Foreword by Valerie Marsch

Copyright © 2023 Mike Kimmel

All rights reserved.
No portion of this book may be reproduced or transmitted in any form or by any means, electronic or mechanical, including photocopying, recording, or by any information storage or retrieval system, except for the inclusion of brief quotations in reviews.

ISBN 978-1-953057-10-5 (paperback)
ISBN 978-1-953057-11-2 (hardcover)
ISBN 978-1-953057-12-9 (ebook)

Library of Congress Control Number 2022917887

Monologues for Young Adults:
60 Original Monologues to Stand Out, Inspire, and Shine
The Professional Actor Series: Book 3

Ben Rose Creative Arts
New York - Los Angeles

Publisher's Cataloging-in-Publication Data
provided by Five Rainbows Cataloging Services

Names: Kimmel, Mike, author. | Marsch, Valerie, writer of foreword.
Title: Monologues for young adults : 60 original monologues to stand out, inspire, and shine / Mike Kimmel ; foreword by Valerie Marsch.
Description: Los Angeles : Ben Rose Creative Arts, 2023. | Series: Professional actor, bk. 3.
Identifiers: LCCN 2022917887 (print) | ISBN 978-1-953057-10-5 (paperback) | ISBN 978-1-953057-11-2 (hardcover) | ISBN 978-1-953057-12-9 (ebook)
Subjects: LCSH: Monologues. | Dramatic monologues. | Acting--Auditions. | Arts--Study and teaching. | Performing arts. | BISAC: PERFORMING ARTS / Monologues & Scenes. | PERFORMING ARTS / Acting & Auditioning.
Classification: LCC PN2080 .K56 2023 (print) | LCC PN2080 (ebook) | DDC 812/.6--dc23.

Interior design by Booknook.biz

Praise for
Monologues for Young Adults

"Love these monologues, and so happy to see them written for adults. This is exactly what actors need when preparing for auditions. I sure hope to see this book at every community theatre, college bookstores, and available online and stores in all of the cities that have TV and film business!"

~ Chuck Disney
 Feature Film Producer
 Film Resource Coordinator,
 Arizona Film Office, Buckeye, Arizona

"This is a fine resource book for actors in college, and in their twenties and thirties. These monologues offer actors a wide variety of opportunities for introspection and deeper-level thinking. I've always admired veteran actors who give something back to newcomers on their way up. Highly recommended for both actors and teachers alike."

~ Linda Ryan
 Owner and Talent Agent,
 Crossbeam Talent Agency, Atlanta, Georgia

"The theater and movie worlds are difficult industries to break into. It requires talent, hard work—and luck. Anyone interested in acting should take advantage of every training and acting opportunity they can. Acting in any legitimate role may catch the eye of a decision maker in the business. Being seen by the right people is crucial, as they must know about you to consider booking you in a future role. Networking with others in the business is also helpful, as they sometimes can suggest someone for a particular role in a project."

> ~ Donna Pedace
> Former Executive Director,
> Eugene O'Neill Theater Center, Waterford, Connecticut

"Strong, introspective, age appropriate monologues that are a great addition to the young actor's library. Each monologue is meaty enough to allow the actor a strong organic performance, without being overly wordy or too lofty. Mike Kimmel's **Monologues for Young Adults** is nice, solid performance material for the young actor."

> ~ GiGi Erneta
> Actress, Radio and TV Host, and Writer
> *Flag of My Father, When the Bough Breaks, Roswell, New Mexico, Veep, The Purge, Nashville, The First, Jane the Virgin, Risen, American Crime, Queen of the South, Scandal, NCIS New Orleans, Dallas, Friday Night Lights, Holiday in Santa Fe*

"I've been a professional actor for 16 years and an acting coach for 5 of those years. I use monologues not only for myself but also for my students to learn and grow. Finding the right monologue is vital! I've seen so many students attempt monologues that are poorly written, have no depth or just not relative. This only ends up hurting the actor. Mike's monologues are not only well written, well thought out and brilliantly constructed but they tell a story. These are all the perfect ingredients for monologues that will make the actor shine! Mike's experience as an actor and in this business is, without a doubt, what makes his monologues so special! Thank you, Mike, for giving actors such an amazing tool to help them find their voice!"

~ April Hartman
Actor and Acting Coach
Reservation Dogs, Queer as Folk, Queen Sugar, One Mississippi, On Becoming a God in Central Florida, Incubus: New Beginnings, Silhouette, Detour, Breakers, Vindication, Amaraica, Forever Red

"Mike Kimmel's **Monologues for Young Adults** is a very helpful resource for young actors in their twenties and thirties. Finding a monologue to perform can be overwhelming. I've personally spent countless hours searching for something unique. **Monologues for Young Adults** has a wide variety of original monologues for actors to choose from for class or auditions. Actors, look no further, you're bound to find a great monologue in this book."

~ Morgan Roberts
Actor-Writer-Director
The Thing About Pam, Girl With a Gun, NCIS: New Orleans, Ravenswood, The Inspectors, My Father Die, The True Don Quixote, When The Game Stands Tall, American Horror Story, Zoo, Dynasty

"The magic of what you want you want in a monologue is right in the pages of the book in your hand. So look no further! Mike Kimmel's Monologues for Young Adults is a captivating collection of ups, downs, highs, and lows of what so many of us go through when going through life at crucial points. Wow! The way he describes his characters' feelings is a new take that I've never seen—but I know I've gone through. In "Get Past Your Past," he says "there's no better time like the present and no better present than your time." It just makes me realize how precious every second we have on this Earth is. It's such a gift! It's a must read that makes you feel connected to how you feel the way you feel. A captivating and inspiring story in every monologue."

> ~ Freddie Ganno
> Actor-Producer
> *Unorganized Crime, Veep, The Deuce, The Tournament, Who Killed Jimmy Gumdrops, The Shades, Bamboo Shark, Mortal Sin, The Demo Crew, Edge City, Twisted Tales*

"With Mike Kimmel's monologues, I can feel confident in knowing I'll be performing an ear-catching piece that will engage the audience in an unexpected way. Not only does it take the actor through a journey of self-discovery, but the listener as well. At times, I found myself experiencing the sensation that Mike had taken my own thoughts and feelings and incorporated them into a monologue while providing valuable insight. It's as if you're getting a life lesson each time you read, study or perform one and, at times, can be transformational. His monologues are entertaining, honest, creative, and packed with inspiration that will definitely grab the listener's attention, which is usually half the battle. In addition to being excellent monologues, they're also great reading to help promote a daily positive mindset and outlook."

> ~ Gwendolynn Murphy
> Dallas Mavericks Dancers Alumni
> Theater, Film and TV Actress
> *The Harrowing, Breakers, Murder Made Me Famous,*
> *Hiding in Plain Sight, No Ordinary Love, Blind Blood,*
> *The Witches of the Watch, Walker, Texas Ranger*

"If you are a person writing a book or trying to write a book, author Mike Kimmel might piss you off because he seems to do it with such ease. He continues to crank them out and they are good. They are uplifting. He seems to know what young people are thinking these days. Mike Kimmel inspires me and I believe he inspires a lot of young people who are looking for good solid monologues."

> ~ Ben McCain
> Actor-Writer-Producer
> *My Name is Bruce, Black Scorpion, Martial Law,*
> *Lois and Clark: The New Adventures of Superman,*
> *Daddy and the Big Boy, Hee Haw, House of Cards,*
> *Killer Tumbleweeds, Bio-Dome, The Tonight Show*

For Chuck and Pam Disney

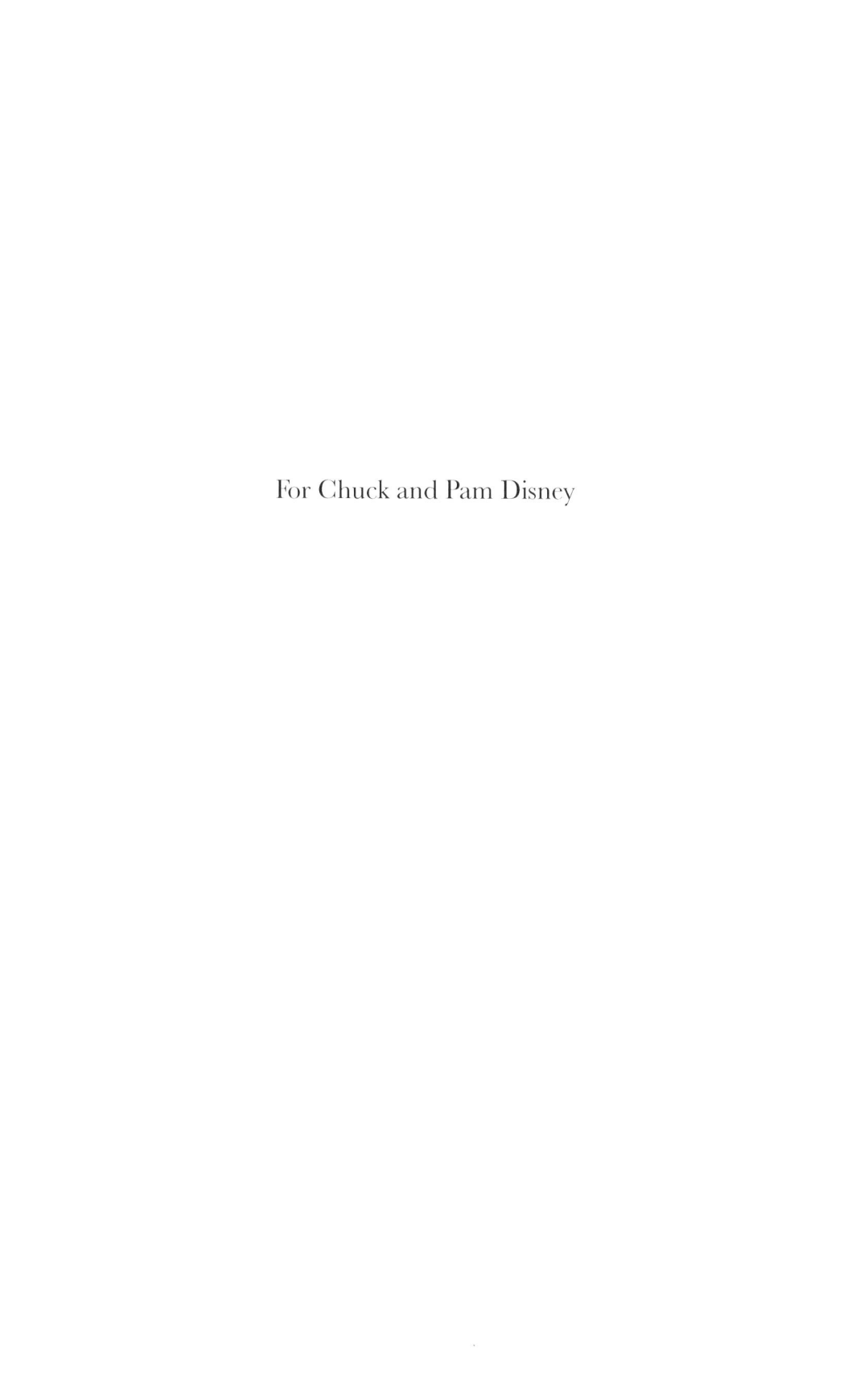

"There are no hopeless situations. There are only men and women who have grown hopeless about them."

~ Marshal Ferdinand Fouche

Table of Contents

Praise for **Monologues for Young Adults**	v
Foreword by Valerie Marsch	xix
Acknowledgments	xxiii
Introduction	xxv
No Competition	1
The Morning Sun	2
Get Past Your Past	3
Every Distraction Gives Me Traction	4
Moving Forward	5
Someday Isle	6
Other People's Drama	7
The Latest Version	8
I Agree	9
The Fine Art of Complaining	10
Self-Fulfilling Prophesy	11
Birds in My Head	12
A Unique Investment Opportunity	14
Junior Year Abroad	16

Semper Gumby	17
Selective Amnesia	18
I Remember Who I Am	19
Rock Star Parking	20
Who Will You Believe?	22
The Flip Side	23
The Other Side of Frazzled	24
Quirks and Eccentricities	25
Have We Met?	26
The Further Down the Road	27
Winter Weight	28
The Biggest Problem	30
I Like Your Mask	32
What You Tolerate	34
My Significant Other	35
The Fault Lies Not in Our Stars	36
Start Where You Stand	37
Choose Pineapple Juice	38
Albert and Marilyn	40
Time and Money	42
Changing, Evolving, and Redirecting	44
One Day or Day One?	45

First Day of the Rest of Your Life	46
Older Than You Think	47
The Wealthiest Places	48
Time Has No Meaning	50
People May Laugh at You	51
A Transactional Process	52
The Difference We Can't See	54
Early Riser	56
Accept and Except	58
The Part That's Not Good	60
The Way Back	62
The More You Know	63
Your Gifts and Talents	64
The Low-Hanging Fruit	66
Hopes, Dreams, and Aspirations	68
The Way of the World	70
Big Plans	72
The Steroid Question	74
Change Your Hat	76
A New Old Friend	78
Time Wounds All Heels	80
The Nicest Man I Ever Knew	82

Mike Kimmel

He Was Gorgeous	84
Post-Pandemic Pleasures	86
Afterword: Two Suggestions on Performance	89
A Request	93
Recommended Reading	94
Performing Arts Books by Mike Kimmel	97
About Valerie Marsch	98
About Mike Kimmel	100

Foreword

I remember the fear this question gave me for years: "Please bring in a monologue so I can see you act, okay?"

First off, for me, finding a monologue was like finding a needle in a haystack. It needs to fit your personality, be of interest to the agent, and show you and your talent in … what, a minute? Reading Mike's book of original monologues for the first time gave me relief, as well as joy. There are so many choices with so much thought in each one and so many styles to pick from. A selection to last a lifetime.

As the writing is new and original, these are, in a sense, specifically written for young adult actors—giving them freedom to create and apply their own unique choices and personal interpretations to the text. I feel this is far more beneficial for the actor, since the agents have not already seen these monologues performed numerous times through the years by a multitude of other actors.

I've been blessed with a very successful career as a model and actor. It was my dream ever since I can remember. As a child, I was always performing around the house, modeling in local shows, reading every fashion book ever printed, and watching my favorite films over and over again to memorize the lines—often to the chagrin of my family and friends!

After finishing up my degree in Fashion Merchandising, I headed straight to New York. I was bold enough to cold-call legendary modeling agent Eileen Ford. I called her seventeen times and was determined not to give up. When I finally got her on the phone, I told her I'm from the midwest, I'm in New York City, and she had to see me and my portfolio! And see me she did. I probably broke all the rules, but my youthful enthusiasm saw me through … and Eileen Ford became my agent, friend, and trusted mentor.

My modeling career took me all over the world and opened up the acting world to me, as well. Models have the job of portraying products—and embodying their essence with their physical poses, facial expressions, style of dress, and the feelings they are able to emote through their eyes and body language. I find acting as "being" the character in a story and taking people out of their everyday lives for a brief period of time. Whether on film, stage, or printed material, the goal is always to get the message and human connection across to your audience.

Lucky for me, I met Mike Kimmel in an acting class at the Screen Actors Guild in New York City. I remember being intrigued by his energy and knowledge. It slipped one day he's a college and university instructor, so it all made sense to me—his reasoning, perception of relationships, and ability to pull material from his brain so others could connect with it and understand.

At this first class, it got even more interesting as he pulled out a tattered ad from a flyer in his pocket. Guess who the model in the ad was? Yes, it was me. I couldn't believe my eyes. He was carrying this tattered ad around, intending to buy the product—an electronics item from an East Coast retail chain, the Wiz, that had just hired me for its latest commercial print campaign. Mike was carrying my picture in his pocket on the day we met. This made us an instant team. We worked together in class that day and have worked together ever since. We eventually formed a weekly "meet group" for actors, a great way to keep informed on the business, and enjoy the camaraderie actors brought to the table … and the fun!

Mike's book of monologues connected with me on a gut level. These monologues gave me a feeling of safety literally in their numbers and with all the creative choices. I have turned my fear into productive time to work on my craft with these monologues right at my fingertips. As we know, we need tools for acting and this book is one of the most important tools available. A must get.

Mike Kimmel has been an inspiration to me since the day we met. Writing a book is so challenging and requires endless hours and devotion. This book is truly a gift for actors of all ages. I also feel that I can speak for others, saying we are grateful for Mike's time, his creative spirit in these choices, and selflessness to push forward and write! And then actually publish the book!

I, for one, am a better actor thanks to Mike Kimmel's monologue books.

Valerie Marsch
New York City

Acknowledgments

As always, a million thanks to my wonderful family—my sisters, their husbands, their children, and children's children, for always being there for me.

Many thanks to Kimberly Bliquez, Susannah Devereux, GiGi Erneta, Katrina Fristoe, April Hartman, Gwendolynn Murphy, Donna Pedace, Linda Ryan, Jeri Slater, Erik Beelman, Jim Blumetti, Stephen Bowling, David Breland, Francis Ford Coppola, Chuck Disney, Freddie Ganno, Ben McCain, Morgan Roberts, Ben Rose, and William Wellman Jr. for their encouragement, support, and expert advice.

Very special thanks to my lifelong friend and colleague, Valerie Marsch, for sharing her personal story in the foreword to this book. Valerie is an immensely talented actor, model, and host. She is also a lady who makes New York a much nicer place to be. I'm grateful for our many years of friendship and collaboration—and especially grateful that she came to class at the Screen Actors Guild that day!

"The secret of getting ahead is getting started."

~ Mark Twain

Introduction: Monologues for Young Adults

Thank you for selecting this book. I hope ***Monologues for Young Adults*** will become a valuable resource that you will refer to often throughout your acting career. My goal in writing this book is for you to find several monologues within its pages that you can relate to—and that will appear to have been written specifically with you in mind.

These monologues are gender-neutral and can be performed by actors of all backgrounds and ethnicities. They are inclusive rather than exclusive. Though this book is intended for actors in their twenties and thirties, it may also be applied to a broader age range. Younger and older actors should be able to find a suitable performance piece here too.

Monologues for Young Adults is the latest in a series of scene, monologue, and instructional books for actors of all ages – child, teen, college, and adult. The reason for this book series is twofold.

First, I believe that actors need a wide range of material to draw upon for professional auditions, class assignments, and weekly solo practice. The sixty original selections in this book should work equally well for each of these three performance scenarios. They are appropriate for both experienced actors and newcomers alike.

Additionally, it's been a personal goal since 2014 to create acting scenes and monologues with uplifting messages, inspiring ideas, and thought-provoking life lessons woven throughout the scripts as subtext. I believe there's a strong need for clean, family-friendly audition material with a positive, optimistic spin for actors of all ages—child, teen, and adult.

My Own Background and Experiences

I've been blessed to work on stage and screen in New York, Los Angeles, and many emerging markets throughout the United States for more than twenty years. I've been fortunate enough to perform lead and supporting roles in feature films, network television, national commercials, theater, sketch comedy, hosting, music videos, corporate training films, and new media projects.

Along the way, I've also worked in a variety of positions behind the scenes. I've been privileged to assist in producing several feature films and was a founding member of a successful theater company. In the process, I've participated in dozens of live casting sessions … and often watched in astonishment as actors talked themselves out of roles they might otherwise have booked. I've cringed while watching actors talk themselves out of opportunities that might have changed the trajectory of their lives and careers.

A Common Trap for Actors

One of the most common ways in which actors sabotage themselves is by gravitating towards wildly inappropriate material in their monologue auditions. I have always believed this is a fundamental—but easily corrected—mistake. Monologues are used in our industry to level the playing field among actors. Monologues show producers and directors how well actors can present themselves with material they've selected and rehearsed on their own. Monologues also give industry professionals an indication of the type of roles actors are drawn towards and wish to perform. Acting teachers and schools often refer to these as "representative roles."

Many actors choose dark, dreary, depressing performance material. Many actors select monologues with violent overtones, inflammatory language, and inappropriate sexual content. Many actors, unfortunately, also seem to carry their own personal black cloud of gloom, pessimism, and negativity everywhere they go. I believe this stems from a desire to brand themselves as "serious, dramatic, edgy" actors who connect deeply with conflict-laden material. When they do so, however, these actors are essentially constructing a concrete wall between themselves and those in a position to hire them.

Actors who audition with dark, argumentative, mean-spirited monologues fail to consider the position of the people they're auditioning for—those industry professionals in a position to hire us. Imagine being a casting director and having to listen to a seemingly endless series of angry, ranting, violent, and inappropriate monologues throughout an all-day-long casting session.

Casting directors, directors, producers, agents, and managers are as human as the rest of us—and can't help but be affected by a barrage of negativity. I once asked a casting director how an actor I recommended had done in his audition. "He gave me a headache," this casting director replied. "The last thing I needed that day was another angry screamer."

A Solution for Actors

It makes far better sense, I believe, to set yourself apart as the actor who shows up for your audition carrying a sense of enthusiasm, hope, and optimism with you. Imagine setting yourself apart from the crowd by presenting yourself as a bright, shining light in a daylong procession of actors bringing anger, cynicism, narcissism, and darkness into the audition room.

This is a subtle "technique" that shows industry professionals you're an actor who understands human nature—and is mature enough to be an effective team player in their production. This is exactly the type of actor producers, directors, and casting directors want to have on their sets. An important component of acting is human psychology—the ability to understand other peoples' wants, needs, and motivations. Actors must remember that although we rehearse and perform monologues alone—we will be part of a larger production ensemble when we're hired. Demonstrating an understanding of our role in this process—and empathy for our collaborators—is an excellent way to separate yourself from the crowd of angry actors auditioning for your role.

Slow Down Your Speech

When practicing and performing these monologues, keep in mind that many actors speak too fast. This is a classic beginners' mistake. I'm always surprised when I see actors rushing to get through their scripts … and then rushing to run out the door. Remember that whenever you're performing a new monologue—it's much newer for your audience. They've never heard it before. If you speak too fast, they can miss an important story point.

You will likely spend considerable time memorizing, practicing, establishing a sense of place, and putting yourself in the proper frame of mind for your monologue audition. Your listeners, however, are hearing these words for the very first time. You must allow directors, producers, casting directors, and audience members ample time to let your words and the storyline of the monologue presented sink in … and then slowly begin to percolate in their minds.

Give the people you're reading for enough time to listen, absorb, and react—just as you would with a scene partner in a two-character dialogue scene. Industry professionals often need a moment to stop, think, and evaluate your performance. They may be trying to think of an adjustment to give you based upon what they've just seen. If they don't say anything right away, it's usually a good sign. They may be trying to figure out where to place you in their project. Don't interrupt producers and directors when they're trying to figure out how to give you a job.

Tame Your Tongue

Besides talking too fast, many actors, unfortunately, talk too much. They talk too much. They talk too fast. They talk too loud. They talk at the wrong time. This is particularly true in the waiting room at auditions. There's a great deal of truth in the old saying: "Silence can never be misquoted."

I've known so many wonderful actors through the years who developed the bad habit of talking too much, talking too loud … and talking about inappropriate topics. They simply could not control their mouths. They said the wrong thing at the wrong time to the wrong person. In the process, they talked themselves out of auditions, bookings, roles, representation, and future opportunities. I knew several brilliant actors who talked themselves right out of the business.

I believe it's vitally important for actors to learn to tame our tongues and quiet those nagging little voices in our heads that speak to us all day long. In doing so, we learn to become our own best friends. We can talk ourselves into victory just as easily as we can talk ourselves into defeat. We must learn to become our most ardent supporters, our most enthusiastic cheerleaders, and the presidents of our very own fan clubs.

Avoid the bad habit of self-deprecating humor too. Don't put yourself down. Don't make jokes at your own expense. There's always a kernel of truth in those negative comments … even when we think we're "just joking." Don't go through life fighting against yourself. Life is too short and the entertainment industry is far too competitive to second-guess yourself and beat yourself up for all your past mistakes and missteps.

When those negative little voices—our uninvited inner critics—start whispering in our ears, we've got to become highly skilled at tuning them out and changing the channel. This is a talent that is well worth developing. It will do you a world of good in every area of your life, both personal and professional.

Fear of Failure. Fear of Success.

The fear of failure is a very real concern in the entertainment industry—and every industry. It prevents people from doing their best by making them hold back. However, I've also seen many actors commit monumental acts of self-sabotage. These experiences have shown me that fear of success holds people back just as often as fear of failure. I've seen many actors show up for auditions who already appeared defeated before they even started to read.

I believe this is much more prevalent in the arts than in other industries primarily because we're working in a qualitative—rather than quantitative—field. Unlike math, science, economics, and engineering, our industry is very subjective. In math, the answer to the problem is always the same. It doesn't change depending upon our feelings. In show business, problem-solving is an entirely different process. The reasons why one actor is hired over another are sometimes difficult to identify and verbalize—even for the person doing the hiring.

On one occasion, I was in the room and heard a young casting director struggle to explain why a certain (and very gifted) actor didn't get the part. His reading was excellent. His credits were solid. His audition skills were top-notch. He was represented by a well-respected agent. The casting director, exasperated, finally explained: "He's just not the guy."

While this can be maddening for the actor who is passed over, it's a longtime reality of our industry. Why is one actor cast as the lead … and the guy who looks just like him cast as his stand-in? It's one of many questions that are difficult to answer in a subjective industry. There are many reasons outside our control why we don't get the job. That's a painful fact. I strongly believe, however, that there are also many times when those same intangible elements will work in our favor, rather than against us. I also believe it's the actor's responsibility to focus solely on the things we can control—and not obsess over all the elements that are out of our control. This brings us to another important point: getting into character.

Getting into Character

Many actors had difficult upbringings—and that's exactly what led them to become actors in the first place. Academy Award winner Gene Hackman noted that "Dysfunctional families have sired a number of pretty good actors." Many actors explain that they were drawn to this business out of a desire to leave their old lives behind and become someone else, someone new, and (presumably) someone better. However, I believe this is a fundamental mistake in approaching our roles, scripts, and audition opportunities.

It's important for actors to keep in mind that we're never *becoming* different people or characters when we audition. Instead, in every role we approach, let's try to imagine how we may portray idealized versions of ourselves in those identical circumstances. These idealized versions of ourselves might be described as the way we present ourselves to others on the best days of our lives. When playing villains, however, the idealized versions of ourselves may be defined by the ways we act out on the *very worst* days of our lives. It's critical to remember, however, that we're always representing distinct aspects of ourselves and our personalities. Therefore, let's try to imagine the best or worst versions of ourselves reacting truthfully to every new set of events and situations offered to us in each new script.

Each of us has multiple aspects of our own personality. Some aspects are good—generous, kindhearted, gracious, well-mannered, and heroic. Others are not so good. When we dig deep, we may recognize aspects of our personalities that are selfish, scheming, and manipulative. It's human nature to see the world in "black or white," "good or bad," and "all or nothing" terms. In reality, though, we don't live in a black and white world. We can more accurately describe the world with varying shades of gray. That's why it's so important not to criticize ourselves too much for past mistakes and errors in communication and judgment. Every mistake from our past is an experience we can now incorporate into the backstories of the characters we play on stage and screen.

We have all stumbled and made mistakes. We have underperformed in every different area of our lives. When we look back on those experiences objectively, we can see that those missteps occurred on days when we were not operating at our very best. The good news is that we're not always going to be that way. We will have plenty of days in the future when we're working at (or near) one hundred percent. As actors, we need to be keen observers of human nature, human experience, and human frailty. The times in life when we've stumbled or fallen can be extremely valuable to us. Our own negative experiences can serve as role models to guide us when portraying "less than ideal" (i.e. flawed or unsavory) characters.

The best way, I believe, to approach every new script and character is to ask yourself: "Which version of myself would be most effective for me in playing this role? What specific past events from my own life—whether positive or negative—can I draw upon to help me breathe life into this character on stage or screen?"

This type of approach to our roles—and our careers—has the added benefit of developing solution-oriented thinking and problem-solving skills. These are vitally important skill sets for performing artists. We all need to be reminded from time to time of the power actors have to affect audiences and bring about positive change, growth, and forward movement in the world.

Reclaim Your Power

As actors, we need to reclaim our power. No matter what happens in the world politically, socially, or economically, there will always be a market for what we do. People will always look to the performing arts not only for entertainment—but also to help interpret and process events transpiring in the world around them. Audiences also look to film, television, theater, and music for the uplifting human connection that strong stories and performances have always provided.

In spite of this, many actors struggle internally with feelings of low self-esteem and self-worth. This is unfortunate (but understandable) given the day-to-day realities of the entertainment industry and its highly competitive nature. I've known so many wonderful actors through the years who quit the business because they were unable to handle the daily grind and frequent rejection. Harrison Ford, looking back on his long, successful mega-career, shared this same experience. "What I observed about my fellow actors," Mr. Ford explained, "was that most gave up very easily."

Possibility vs. Probability

That's why it's so important for us to focus on possibilities, rather than probabilities. When actors focus their attention on probabilities, they're looking at the vast number of people auditioning for each new role. They're looking at the relatively low percentage of people who are able to book substantial roles and build solid careers. They're looking at the small number of people who are able to stay in the business through the years and through the decades—without becoming bitter, jaded, and damaged. With this type of focus, it's very easy to become overwhelmed and demoralized.

When actors focus on possibilities, however, they open their minds up to the greater achievements available to all of us. If a well-known actor has accomplished something you admire, then that proves it's possible for all of us. Success always leaves visible clues. Maybe we can all find encouragement in identifying the actors who have come from circumstances similar to our own—and have achieved incredible success.

I am not advocating a Pollyanna attitude towards our careers—but it's very important to give ourselves a pep talk now and then. I've heard motivational speakers tell us that we can do anything. Well, I don't believe we can do anything—but I believe we can accomplish extraordinary things when we're operating in the areas of our strongest gifting, interest, and dedication. For example, I've always enjoyed playing basketball. If I practice basketball for twelve hours a day, I know I'll improve. I also know I'll never be good enough to play in the NBA. If I put that same time and effort into acting and writing, however, my opportunities for success are multiplied a thousand-fold. In and out of the entertainment industry, I've seen people accomplish incredible things when they focus their attention on the areas in which they're most qualified.

Remember this principle. In spite of the odds, it's possible. We cheer for the underdog in movies, but very few people are willing to step into that underdog role in real life. Most people on Earth prefer to play it safe. This is understandable. It's difficult to venture outside of our comfort zones. But major achievements usually don't happen for us inside our comfort zones. Academy Award winner Angelina Jolie said it best: "If you don't get out of the box you've been raised in, you won't understand how much bigger the world is."

The Best Reason to Persevere

I was hired several times to teach beginner acting classes for older adults—women and men in their sixties, seventies and eighties. Their personal stories were always the same. These senior citizens told me that they wanted to get started and pursue careers in show business when they were eighteen, nineteen, or twenty. Family, friends, co-workers, and romantic partners talked them out of it. They then gravitated towards other fields, settled down, and raised families. Along the way, they often asked themselves: "What if?"

Fifty years later, they showed up in acting class wondering how their lives might have been different had they acted upon their youthful desires. Sometimes, the people closest to us can keep us from moving forward in life and achieving our maximum potential. Some of us may need to distance ourselves from well-meaning dream stealers and dream killers. Unfortunately, some of us may also have people in our inner circles that do not truly have our best interests at heart.

I've heard it said there are two types of pain in life: the pain of discipline and the pain of regret. I believe the best reason to pursue your show business dreams as a young adult is to save your future self fifty years of regret and unanswered questions. The years will pass no matter what you do. Don't let them pass you with regrets.

The Best Reason to Quit

Besides teaching seniors, I've had the experience of teaching acting for younger ages: children, teens, and adults. As adults, it's possible you'll pursue an acting career enthusiastically for a time—and then recognize that show business is not the right career path for you. That's okay. I've seen many fine actors make that decision.

Let me share one of my favorite teaching stories. I once had an eight-year-old acting student tell me: "I'd like to be in a movie if someone wants to put me in there, but I don't want to memorize all these lines. That's boring." Obviously, acting was not the right choice for this youngster. Actors always have to memorize lines. That's not going to change anytime soon, so I think it's terrific when one of my classes (or books) helps people decide NOT to move forward with their acting careers.

I believe if you pursue this industry wholeheartedly—and then decide that it's just not for you—then you're very fortunate to have figured that out early in life. You can save yourself many regrets and "what if's" when you're older. I believe the best reason to step away from this industry is that you've tried it, given it your all, and just don't enjoy the lifestyle. There's no shame in that. It's nothing to be embarrassed about. The auditioning, uncertainty, and frequent rejection, quite honestly, are pretty tough for all of us—even star-name actors.

Your Next Step

I've always loved the expression: "Give it the old college try." If you feel inspired to pursue an acting career, then I encourage you to take off the training wheels and chase your dream in earnest. Learn some new monologues. Get in a good class. Practice with a scene partner. Network with other actors. Build your credits with student films and community theater. Find an agent. Take a casting director workshop. Join a theater company. Get involved with a filmmaking group. Make your own short films. Write yourself a one-person show. There are a hundred things you can do to build your credits and your career without having to ask anyone's permission. Along the way, you'll gain valuable experience and figure out if this industry is right for you.

Logically, I think it makes good sense to throw yourself fully into the mix, and then decide if this is a place where you want to be. I'm not telling you it's going to be easy. I'm telling you it's going to be worth it. Success is never convenient. It takes courage, discipline, and a VERY thick skin to pursue your dream enthusiastically while tuning out all the background noise around you.

I hope these monologues will resonate deeply with you and help you to reach the next level in your acting career. I wish you all the very best of happiness, health, and success in pursuing this worthy goal and wild adventure.

Stay strong.

Mike Kimmel
Los Angeles, California

"To lead an orchestra, you must turn
your back on the crowd."

~ Aristotle

No Competition

Call me a rebel, but I like to see people happy and successful. Life should be a beautiful journey … not a no-holds-barred fight to the finish.

Therefore, I am not even remotely interested in competing with you. Zero interest in competition. Because if we took the time and energy we wasted by comparing ourselves with others … and invested it in improving ourselves instead … we would all be much happier and more successful. And a million times more productive.

Grandpa used to tell me that if we work hard at becoming the best possible versions of ourselves, then we won't really have any competition. Unless we create it for ourselves—and who in their right mind wants to do that?

Listen. There's only one way I want to compete against you … and that's through my actions articulated on your behalf. Wanna test me on this? Fine. Go ahead. Try me. Throw down that gauntlet.

Treat me as well as you possibly can. Do your best. Build the best you. Become the friendliest, kindest, most gracious, most helpful and magnanimous version of yourself that you can ever hope to be. Be as nice as you can be to me.

And I promise you … I will treat you ten times better.

The Morning Sun

My mind's been working overtime lately. Too much stress. Too little peace. Been thinking way too much … and thinking about some things it would be better to forget.

I think about jobs I've had and lost. Places I've lived and left. Opportunities that have come and gone. And the significant other who should have become my one and only … all those years ago.

I think about my victories and I think about my defeats, but I try to think about my victories more. Most days I'm successful in that quest. Other days … not so much.

But I give thanks every morning for the rising of the sun … and the opportunity it brings to put on my battle armor, venture out into this cold, hard, beautiful world … and try once more.

Because the sunshine doesn't care what you did in the moonlight. Doesn't ask how many times you cried yourself to sleep. The sun is a gentleman and doesn't keep score.

I've found that the morning sun is also very forgiving. It never holds a grudge. The morning sun forgives us every day for yesterday's mistakes and transgressions. It always brings us another chance to get up, get out, get it together, and get it right.

Get Past Your Past

I've got a challenge for you today. I challenge you to get past your past. We've all been kicked around a time or two in this beautiful little game called "Life." I get it. I've been there myself. More times than I care to remember.

Hemingway said that the world breaks everybody… and many are strong at the broken places.

I've found that healing old wounds is sometimes easier said than done. But if you don't heal from the things that hurt you, you'll bleed all over people who didn't cut you.

Maybe we're too trusting. And it's good to be trusting, but it's best to be trusting to those who've earned your trust. And I still … even after everything that's happened to me … believe people should help one another. Don't wait. There's no better time than the present … and no better present than your time.

So my advice is this: Don't go through life with a cold, raging, and bitter heart. Forget your past enough to get over it, but remember it enough to make sure it never happens to you again. Pack it up. Wrap it up tight and put it away. Move on.

Dedicate your daily future to getting past your distant past.

Mike Kimmel

Every Distraction Gives Me Traction

Who are you? Yeah, that's right. I'm talking to you. I ask who you are because I want to know if we're alike. I wonder how much you're just like me.

Let me share something with you. I've kinda had an issue in my life with procrastination and distraction. Maybe you've been there yourself.

But what's more important than where we've been is where we're going now. And I've learned to move away from distraction and procrastination. I've learned to tame those two little mental beasts.

Because, let's face it, distractions can be fun. A friend invites you to lunch. A new video game comes out. Your favorite show comes on TV. Hey, I get it.

I've had the experience of being distracted a few times. Maybe a few hundred times. But we all know what we need to do in life. We don't need a counselor or life coach to tell us everything, right? Deep down, we all know what we need to do to become who we need to be.

So keep your distractions to a minimum. Better still, when a distraction comes along, I use it as a warning bell to remind me what I need to do. What I need to roll up my sleeves and finish. I've learned to use these distractions that come up as an extra incentive to stay on track and keep on working on what I need to keep on working on.

Nowadays, every distraction gives me traction.

Moving Forward

Can I ask you a very personal question? How did you get here today? How did you arrive at this particular juncture in time, space … and eternity?

Let's start small, shall we? Let's get really micro. Did you walk here? Did you take the train? Did you take the bus?

You drove? Great. Can you tell me about the windshield in your car? That's right, the windshield. Is it big or small? Okay. Big. That's what I thought.

How about your rear-view mirror? Big or small? Small. Great.

Why is your windshield big and your rear-view mirror small? Because where you're going is so much more important than where you've been. My car's got the same set-up too, by the way. It reminds me every day that reaching my destination point down the road is much more important than revisiting every place I've already been on this lifelong journey of mine.

Maybe you can relate. We all have somewhere to go in life, a destination specifically meant for each of us. But we have to guard that goal, be protective of that journey … and not find ourselves distracted by every shiny new object that crosses the road ahead of us. Because even if we stay on the right track, there are many tempting parking spaces for us along the way to divert our attention and take us off course. So keep moving forward. Always keep moving forward.

Someday Isle

I was born on a tropical island. I spent most of my life there. Someday Isle. Maybe you know the place. A lot of people like me spent way too many years there. Wasted too many years there.

Someday, I'll go back to school and finish that degree. Someday, I'll launch that new business. Someday, I'll write that book. Someday, I'll pick up a guitar and teach myself to play. You might say I was living on Someday Isle.

Like I said, I spent way too many years there. Until I woke up one day. I woke up and realized I had spent most of my life half-asleep. Finally, I got out of that too-comfortable place and that no-movement life situation. I finally found the courage and strength to vote myself off that island. And I strongly suggest you do the same.

Buddha said that the problem is simple. We all think we have time. But remember that the clock is always ticking … for every one of us. Be careful with the dreams you've been given. Be careful with your gifts and talents too. Be careful not to dock your boat on Someday Island. Be careful not to someday your life away.

Other People's Drama

I'm here to give you some unsolicited advice. Keep your eyes open. Be extremely careful about who you allow into your inner circle.

Don't let people pull you into their drama. And don't let them define your character. Most importantly, don't accept their definition of who you're supposed to be. Because every one of us is the villain in someone else's story.

And if you've been burned before—like most of us have—make up your mind to never let yourself be burned by the same flame twice. You can't control other people, but that's something you can control. You always have a choice what to believe about yourself, your capability, and your destiny.

Because every day you're being presented with two options: evolve or repeat. You can choose Door Number One or Door Number Two.

And in order to evolve into the optimal version of myself, I have to tune out the background noise of other people's drama.

So I'm learning. I'm becoming really good at multi-tasking too. Nowadays, I can listen, ignore, and forget all at the same time.

The Latest Version

I had an argument with my old college roommate. Not an argument, exactly, but we definitely saw things from two different points of view.

Weird thing to disagree on too. You know what it was all about?

Phones. Yeah, phones.

My friend got all snippy with me over my phone. Really went off. That it's so old, not the latest version, doesn't have all the new upgrades. All the bells and whistles.

What a thing for someone to get an attitude about! Because my phone is just a tool. That's how I see it. I use it for two things. Telephone calls and emails. I'm not even a big texter, to tell you the truth. That's the biggest time waster of the twenty-first century. Maybe any century. People use that texting feature way too much. It's a deep, dark vortex that sucks away people's time, attention, and energy.

No, thank you. I'm much more interested in face-to-face, up close, and personal interactions. Human interactions. I'm protecting myself from things that misdirect my time, energy and focus.

I'd rather focus on my own new and improved latest version … rather than that of my devices. I'm focusing on achieving … by actively creating … my own personal best. I'm upgrading to my very own 2.0.

I Agree

Agree with what's good. Disagree with what's … not so good. Do you agree with that philosophy?

I stand in agreement with my Daily Best … not my Daily Beast.

And that, my friends, is the secret to happiness and fulfillment. Being in full, one hundred percent agreement with the very best possible future versions of ourselves.

But it's not always easy. Because when we're out there in the world … working, going to school, interacting with friends, family, strangers … we're constantly bombarded by a wide variety of things from both sides of the spectrum … the best of the best and the worst of the worst.

We have two voices talking to us all day long. The positive and the negative. The selfish and the selfless. The mean-spirited and the kindhearted. Which one will you choose to listen to? Where will you put your full attention? The choice is always up to us. Every day it's a battle between our best and worst, the highest and lowest aspects of our nature.

I don't know about you, but I've found that I am always happiest … and I am always at my best … when I stand in full agreement with the very best of all possible versions of myself.

Here's my advice for working our way through all that background noise that comes our way daily. Remember who it is you want to be. Focus, aim, and project yourself towards the ideal version of you. Agree with your best. Disagree with your worst. Boom. Done.

Mike Kimmel

The Fine Art of Complaining

I've been hearing too much complaining lately. I know we all make that mistake from time to time, but some people act like they're going for the blue ribbon. Here's the rule: If you complain about something more than three times, you're not looking for a solution, you're looking for attention.

Are things gonna happen in life that we have a reason to complain about? Yes, of course they will. But it's the excessive amount of complaining that some people get trapped in that is really the problem for most of us.

When you're tempted to start complaining, ask yourself instead, "Does anyone ever get anything from their complaining? Do they receive any practical benefit or are they just complaining to hear themselves talk? And hear themselves squawk.

When I was a kid growing up, I used to hear adults say that the squeaky wheel gets oiled. But now that I'm an adult, out in the job market, at least, I find that the squeaky wheel actually gets replaced. That's a lesson for all of us to remember.

Nobody wants to hear complaining even when there's something tangible to complain about.

I don't want to hear complaining ever, from anyone ... including myself. I don't even like to hear myself complain about how much other people out in the world complain.

Self-Fulfilling Prophesy

You know, I always thought I wasn't mechanically inclined. I used to think I'm just not good at it. Building stuff, fixing stuff … I thought I wasn't good at it.

One time, when I was trying to put a piece of furniture together, my ex told me that I'm about as handy as a foot. Now you can see why this person is my ex. So, because of hearing things like that all my life, that thought was embedded in my consciousness. This is not my skill set. I'm not good at it. I self-identified as a person who is not mechanically inclined.

But then we learned in psychology class that's called a self-fulfilling prophesy. In other words, if you think that way, it's going to cause you to act in ways that are consistent with that belief. Because human beings crave consistency. We want to act out in ways that are congruent with our deeply-held belief patterns.

That's why it's so important never to speak out anything negative about yourself. It's important never to speak out something that you don't want to be true. Because we can then … subconsciously … begin to act in ways that make that idea become real in our lives. That's how our words can cause our inner beliefs to become our outer reality.

Is this making any sense to you? I hope so. Because I self-identify as a person who makes a lot of sense.

Mike Kimmel

Birds in My Head

You know what my father said? My father said I had birds in my head. He meant well. He always means well. We just disagreed on the plans I had for my future.

Dad wanted me to carry a leather briefcase. Get a good, stable corporate job. House in the suburbs. White picket fence.

All of which is fine, by the way. None of which is me, by the way.

My father and I disagreed about the plans I had for my future. He had wonderful plans, but it was my future. My plans, you see, were a little less stable, a little less predictable, a little less secure.

I wanted to be an artist. That's all I ever dreamed of since I was five years old. A full-time career in the arts. Music, writing, painting, drawing, singing, dancing, comedy, drama. All of the above. That's all I wanted to do ever since I can remember. The only subjects I was interested in all through school.

Biggest fight I ever had with my father. He screamed like a banshee. Told me I was throwing my life away, wasting the good college education he worked so hard to provide, and bringing shame on our family name.

There didn't seem to be any room for compromise. No middle ground between us. That's a conundrum. I get it. But I'm happy to report that with the check I just received from the National Arts Foundation, along with the grant from my alma mater, and the last three months of royalty checks for my breakthrough project … no middle ground is going to be necessary.

Those payments totaled out to … more money than I ever thought I would see at one time in one place in my lifetime. More money than I knew what to do with. But I figured out what to do with it.

My father screamed like a banshee when he opened the letter. The satisfaction of mortgage letter from his bank … telling him that his thirty-year home loan has now been paid in full. And after he screamed, he cried like a baby. My father cries every time he tells that story now. Because, in spite of all our differences, nobody could be happier for me than my dear old dad.

I guess those birds in my head turned out to be carrier pigeons. They delivered a very important message to my father. It's the same message that's been bouncing around inside my head since I was five years old. The white picket fence is optional. It will always be there for you. Following your dreams … and dedicating your life to quenching that raging fire in your belly … is never optional. It's always mandatory.

Mike Kimmel

A Unique Investment Opportunity

I was invited to participate in a unique new investment opportunity. They want me to help fund their project. Had a whole presentation. Put together a nice package. Fancy gold-embossed folders and everything. They even said we would be like a part of the family if we joined. That was the deal breaker for me.

Part of the family? What kind of family are we talking about here? Little House on the Prairie or the Manson family? There's a lot of wiggle room between those two goalposts … and a lot of opportunity for miscommunication. And maybe misrepresentation.

Anyway, there were a lot of non-specifics going on there … at this unique investment opportunity. Quite a bit happening that I'm not too sure about. Example: how do they determine when they've broken even? And then turned a profit? And how much of that profit are they going to turn over to their investors? When do the investors break even?

How do I know they're not keeping two sets of books? Who's watching the bottom line? Who's protecting my money? Yes, I know they've got an accountant, but who's supervising the accountant?

As they wrapped up this unique investment opportunity meeting, they told us that if we move quickly, we can all get in on the ground floor. As I recall from my last unique investment opportunity, the ground floor is exactly where you don't want to be when the roof caves in. And that's exactly what happened to me last time … with the last group of people who told me I could join their family.

So I think I'll pass on this unique investment opportunity. Grandpa ... the grandfather in my real family ...used to say that the only guaranteed way to double your money is to fold it in half and put it back in your pocket. I'm keeping the nice, fancy gold-embossed folder though.

And I'm also keeping my hard-earned, highly-sought-after, cold, hard cash. Right here in my pocket where it belongs. Folded and doubled for safe-keeping ... just like my real family taught me.

Junior Year Abroad

My friends and family tried to talk me out of it. The junior year abroad program at my college. I spent my junior year halfway across the world in a foreign country. It was a big step … and a little scary. Okay, a lot scary. But I'm glad I didn't listen to all the advice from family and friends. Glad I didn't listen to the nay-sayers. Because this big step turned out to be the best decision I ever made.

It wasn't easy, of course. Nothing about it was easy. Learning a new language, learning how to get around, learning a new currency. I had to immerse myself, jump in and learn all the social, cultural, and national differences too. Plus, I had to learn a thousand and one other things I could never have anticipated.

Sound overwhelming? That's because it was overwhelming.

But this was my takeaway. It doesn't matter what I might have expected … or failed to expect. Because I learned something about myself … and my own level of adaptability. Apparently, I am one extremely flexible and resourceful human being. That's great to know. It's one of those things I couldn't have predicted … but it's been a discovery that will serve me well no matter where I go in this big, beautiful world … and even if I choose to stay right in the quiet of my own little neighborhood. Right here in the quiet of my own home town … with all the well-meaning nay-sayers who told me not to go away.

Semper Gumby

I'm ex-military. Combat veteran too. Three tours. That changes a person, no matter what they tell you when you get home.

Stepping back into civilian life now. I was pretty young when I enlisted.

Wasn't exactly sure what to expect when I joined the military. But whatever I did expect … whatever I might have believed to be true … let's just say … I was wrong. Because things changed over there on a daily basis. So all of us had to learn to adapt.

Semper Gumby. That was our slogan. You've probably heard "Semper Fi," but I'll bet you never heard "Semper Gumby." That means always flexible … like Gumby. Ready to twist yourself into any new position and go in any new direction … and always ready to bounce back into your original shape, reclaim your power, and start all over again. No matter what the world may throw at you. Semper Gumby.

That uncertainty is what changes a person most. It develops you. It fills you up. It fills you out. In the process, it fills up all the places inside that you once believed were empty.

And that's the best lesson I learned from being ex-military. The most valuable lesson you can learn … and can apply … once you bounce back into your original position, reclaim your power … and step back into civilian life.

Selective Amnesia

Can I share a secret? I have a longtime friend who has developed a little bit of an issue. Selective amnesia.

Only remembers things that are convenient. What's not convenient, my friend discards. Example. She doesn't remember borrowing money from me. Which is pretty convenient, because if you don't remember borrowing the money, then you won't have to remember to pay it back.

That works out pretty nicely now, doesn't it?

Yeah, yeah, I know. Some people just aren't good with their money. I get that. Totally get it. But this friend isn't good with my money, either. And that's against the rules.

My Uncle Charlie warned me about this many years ago. He told me to expect that anyone who asks to borrow money is never going to pay it back. Maybe they have good intentions when they ask … or maybe they have bad intentions when they ask. Doesn't matter. The result is still the same. There's never a boomerang effect. That cash never makes a return trip.

So when you lend money to a friend … don't ever expect to see that money again. And if you hold them accountable … and ask for your money back … then don't ever expect to see that friend again.

You'll have to train yourself to forget that friend. And that will be your own opportunity to practice selective amnesia.

I Remember Who I Am

I forgot something very important. I forgot who I am. I forgot who I'm supposed to be. I'm supposed to be the person others can count on … to make a difference. A difference with my family, a difference with my friends, and a difference in the world.

But I've noticed lately that there have been many times when I didn't do that. I wasn't there for the people who depended on me. The ones who needed me most. Maybe it was selfishness. Maybe it was ego. Maybe it was a "what's in it for me" attitude rearing its ugly head. Maybe it was all of the above.

But it doesn't matter because those opportunities to make a real difference are now gone. Those ships have sailed, never to be boarded again. And some of those people I should have blessed have now departed, as well.

I can't say I didn't think of blessing them … because I did. I thought about performing certain acts of kindness and generosity but I failed to act on those impulses. I didn't follow through. I didn't make those calls. I didn't send those checks. I didn't deliver those gifts. And now it's too late.

But it wasn't in vain. There will be other opportunities to bless someone with a selfless act in the future. Someone. Somewhere. Somewhen. I hope so, anyway. And when those new opportunities present themselves … I'll remember the lesson. I'll remember the opportunity cost from all the moments I missed. And I'll remember every unfulfilled yesterday that has come and gone. Because now I remember who I am.

Mike Kimmel

Rock Star Parking

I was running late today. Got myself all stressed out. So crazed. That's not like me. I'm usually much better organized. Totally on it. Never late.

Because I know if I'm late to that first appointment … it's all downhill after that. The Domino Theory of Cause and Effect. That first instance of lateness generates twelve additional latenesses subsequently. Like a great big evil snowball rolling downhill, gathering momentum, obliterating my day slowly but surely, inch by inch, minute by minute on its venomous downward spiral. Maybe you're experienced this phenomenon yourself.

Being late to the first meeting makes me late to the next … and the next after that, ad infinitum. And every single person at every single point is now mad at me … and rightfully so … because I fouled up all of their schedules too.

Been down this road before. Been there, done that, got the T-shirt. So I gave up. Figured there's no sense fighting it. Made up my mind to stop rushing. Show up when I can. Get there when I get there … and take my well-deserved lumps.

So I drove up to my first appointment … fully prepared to circle the block for ten minutes looking for parking … as usual. And much to my surprise … Boom! Found a spot right in front of the door … with forty minutes on the meter. Rock star parking and I didn't even have to pay. Not what I expected from past experience.

Walked in and discovered the guy I was meeting was running late too! He was so stressed out. Totally humble and apologetic. Asked if we could please reschedule for next week when he'll have more time … and be better organized.

That works. Got back in the car and was right on schedule. Ahead of schedule, actually. All that stress, angst, and worry … for nothing. Like it never happened.

What's my takeaway? Show up and try even when you're not at your best. When it looks like circumstances are not in your favor. There may be a lot of things going on behind the scenes that we can't predict. Show up even when you don't feel like it. Because nobody knows how you feel. How you feel is irrelevant. So you may as well act calm and confident when you show up. You'll calm down the people around you … and you may even calm yourself down too.

Who Will You Believe?

Who will you believe?

Someday, you will believe someone ... and the person you choose to believe on that day will determine who you become for the rest of your life.

So who will you believe?

Will you believe the people living in fear? People so afraid of making a mistake that they never step out of their comfort zones? Some people go through their whole lives like timid little jackrabbits terrified of their own shadows. They're so afraid to do the wrong thing that they never do anything.

Or will you believe the people stuck in the past? Those who spend their days and nights replaying the mental movies of every negative event, unfortunate circumstance, and catastrophic interaction they've experienced since childhood? Tony Robbins says the past has no power over us unless we choose to live there.

Most people spend their lives either re-living the past or running away from the future. That's why they're never able to experience happiness and fulfillment in the present day moment. But that's really the only moment we ever have available to us.

So think long and hard about who you're going to believe in life. Whose advice you're going to take. Whose lead you're going to follow.

And never waste one more beautiful today beating yourself up for yesterday or trying to hide yourself away from tomorrow.

The Flip Side

I try to do things different. Differently, actually. Differently is correct grammar. And a lot of people my age don't pay attention to their grammar. Not me. I like to be different.

Not because I like grammar. Nobody likes grammar.

But because I like to use my head. I like to think for myself. That's why I try to look at things in a different kind of way. Different than most people on Planet Earth. Not just accept at face value all the things everyone tells me are supposed to be true.

That's being an individualist. That's being a forward thinker. That's using my critical thinking and problem solving skills. And isn't that … kinda what we're supposed to do in life? Think for ourselves? I think so.

But on the flip side, a lot of people feel threatened when you ask the hard questions. Maybe they feel disrespected. Like I'm being disrespectful if I ask the "why" questions and try to think for myself. But what they see as disrespect is my desire to delve deeply into a new realm. The realm of clear thinking, objectivity, and problem solving.

Not just following the crowd in all I think and say and do. Because, when you get right down to it, thinking for yourself is kinda like the flip side of being a robot. And nobody wants to live their life like a robot. Not even a robot.

Mike Kimmel

The Other Side of Frazzled

Can I tell you a secret? I used to be a little bit stressed. High-strung. Had a bad temper too. I would fly off the handle at the slightest provocation. And, believe me, all I have to do is walk out of my apartment … and I have plenty of slightest provocations.

Not a good way to go through life. Not a good recipe for success.

My sister used to say I looked … "frazzled" … like a bundle of nerves. Like that mad scientist in *Back to the Future* with the wild eyes and the crazy hair.

Then I had an epiphany. Frazzled is not helpful to me. Because I can't do the things I want to do in that crazed state of mind. I can't be effective when I'm spending all my time, effort and energy over-reacting to every idiotic, insignificant little thing that my better judgment tells me I should ignore.

So ignoring is what I'm doing now. Learning to ignore has become my new personal antidote. Ignoring is the flip side of that old frazzled coin. Now I flip it. I can flip that coin. Because ignoring is the other side of frazzled.

Quirks and Eccentricities

I have some personal quirks and eccentricities. Maybe you can relate. I don't do the things other people like to do. I do the things I like to do.

If a crowd of people goes left, I go right. A wise man said, "Do not try to follow the beaten path. Go instead where there is no path and make the path where you walk."

That's my new motto. That's my goal, destination and guiding point (in life) these days. To walk my own walk, talk my own talk, and make my own path through this weird, wonderful world we call home.

My path may not be right for you, but that's okay. They're my feet, not yours. I'm the one who's gotta shoe 'em, keep 'em smelling good and fresh, and point them in the right direction.

And I've learned to recognize when I'm walking in the right direction. Because there's never any traffic. The beaten path is smoother and better paved, but the traffic's terrible.

Maybe you think I'm being anti-social … and that's okay. I get it. Because it's not your job to like me, appreciate me, respect me, and approve of all my choices in life.

It's my job to like me, appreciate me, respect me, and approve of all my choices in life.

Have We Met?

Have we met? No, I don't believe we have. I'm the new version of me. I've been around a while, but you might say I've been hidden behind the scenes. Hiding behind the version of myself that the outside world has previously gotten to know. That's the old me.

The good news is … those days are over. Subjugated no more to the world's false beliefs, idea patterns, and cardboard standards. Never again a prisoner of group think.

You see, I've done a great deal of reconstructive work. You might say I've completely reinvented myself. Now I have absolutely nothing in common with that earlier model … that person you used to know … back in the old days. Except of course that the two of us are exactly the same person.

Physically, at least. Our DNA is a pretty close match. Identical, in fact. I'd say identical is a pretty close match, right? But I'd like to think our similarity ends there.

Because I will no longer fall prey to the miscommunications, errors in judgment, societal pressures, and conformity that once defined my relationships with others. And my relationship with myself. I'm bound and determined to avoid all those old missteps, misrepresentations, false beliefs, and narrow-minded thinking. I can't promise I'll do it one hundred percent, but that's the new goal.

So … I'll ask you one more time. Have we met? Because if you haven't met me lately, I can promise you … you don't know me at all.

The Further Down the Road

Do you ever feel like you've gone too far down the road? Past the point of no return?

Well, I've been there too. And I don't believe there's a hopeless case out there in the world. Nobody is ever so far gone that they can't find their way back home again.

There's a lot of people who feel hopeless these days. You know how I know that? Because I have proof. Documentation. It's always been that way … throughout all the centuries of human existence. The more things change, the more things remain the same. Hemingway wrote about it a hundred years ago. Epictetus wrote about it a thousand years ago.

We might have better technology than they did, but human beings haven't changed at all. Sometimes, our thoughts and actions can lead us to some pretty dark places. That's when we need to stay hopeful the most.

And it's a funny thing about hope. They say that hope never abandons us … but sometimes we abandon hope. That's a choice. That's on us. So don't ever give up hoping and believing for something better.

Keep a spirit of hope alive in your heart daily. You're never so lost that you can't be found. Because the further down the road you go, the closer you get to finding your way back home again. Finding your way right back to where you belong. Finding your way back to where you're always supposed to be.

Mike Kimmel

Winter Weight

Don't say it. I know what you're thinking. It looks like I've put on a few pounds since last time you saw me. Winter weight.

But that's not actually true. My weight is exactly proportional to my height. I just happen to be much taller than I look. I'm really seven foot ten. In my stocking feet, I'm seven foot eleven. I wear very thick socks.

I know. I know. I don't look that tall to you … but I am. You're not seeing me accurately. You're seeing me subjectively. You're experiencing an optical illusion, caused in part by the inconsistent refraction of light coming through that little window over there.

As light shines through the window, it bends and curves and becomes rounded. It then gives the impression that my torso is rounded … and slightly more curved than it actually is in nature. That's physics, the science of physical processes. You're welcome.

If this is slightly confusing to you, don't be embarrassed. Science was never my best subject, either. Until I enrolled in culinary school … and chose desserts as my specialty. Studying the chemical composition of all my favorite cream sauces, puddings, and cake frostings has helped me appreciate the role chemistry plays upon our understanding of the physical world in which we live. And eat. And eat and eat and eat.

And it's not only physics and chemistry. Psychology teaches us that inside every heavy person is a skinny person trying to get out. But I've found that I can usually silence that skinny person with a nice, thick slice of strawberry cheesecake. With two dollops of my award-winning, homemade salted caramel whipped cream on top. And, uh ... maybe a second slice of cheesecake ... just to make sure I got the recipe right.

How about you? How do you silence that skinny person ... and that inner critic ... inside of you?

Mike Kimmel

The Biggest Problem

Today was an okay day. Not my best, but definitely better than my worst. I was thinking about my grandmother a lot. It's been six months now and I still can't believe I'm never gonna see her again.

I was very close with my grandmother. I guess you figured that out already. Sometimes, when I would have a bad day, I would pick up the phone and call. She always talked so nice and so sweet to me. She had so much patience and always gave me such good advice.

Just this morning I went to call her … and then I remembered. Guess I don't have her phone number any more.

But you know what? I talked with her enough times that I know what she would have said to me. I can figure out her advice.

Grandma had a great saying whenever I was stressed. She used to say, "I hope this is the biggest problem you'll ever have in your life." She must have said that a million times. Such a simple message … and yet containing so much wisdom. This was her way of giving people a broader view … so they can understand the context of what they're going through. Showing us that what we're dealing with is not really so catastrophic … and we can get through it just like we've worked through all our other problems in life.

Grandma went through a lot of difficult situations. I guess that's where her sense of perspective came from. That was my grandmother's superpower.

Next time you feel frustrated or frazzled, remember this. Very few of us are ever greatly wronged in life … or thrown into horrific circumstances that we didn't deserve … and are beyond our control. Learn to keep the big picture in mind, keep your head on straight … and establish your practical frame of reference.

Remember the good advice and the worldly-wise perspective of my grandmother with her fourth grade education. "I hope this is the biggest problem you'll ever have."

I Like Your Mask

I'm so glad we're done with all that craziness.

Do you remember those days? Maybe I'm remembering all that mess worse than it really was … because we tend to embellish in retrospect.

But I don't believe that's what's happening here. I remember it being pretty awful. And … I believe I'm remembering things exactly as they were. The pandemic, the quarantine, the virus, the vaccine … and mostly all the fear. Most of all, I remember the fear, dread, and hopelessness we saw all around us.

Everyone I knew was looking for some kind of bright spot … but there didn't ever seem to be one. Nobody I knew could find anything to be happy or grateful about during that horribly difficult time. Not even vaguely optimistic.

Except my Uncle Jake. My dad's big brother. Sixty years old and still going strong.

Uncle Jake was a lifelong bachelor. Never got married. Never found the right lady. He dated. He had girlfriends. Never seemed to find the right one. And the right one never seemed to find him.

But that's okay, he always said. Nobody's one hundred percent. Nobody's firing on all cylinders in every area of their life. And Uncle Jake had plenty of other areas of his life that were going well. So he chose to focus on those things instead.

Friends. Sports. Health and fitness. And his work. Uncle Jake was very passionate about his work. And one day, during that crazy time, a lady walked into his shop wearing a strange looking mask. Same size and shape as the normal, assembly line masks, but with a very unusual pattern.

Uncle Jake, gentleman that he is, complimented this woman on her mask. Never thought we'd get to the point where we're complimenting strangers on their masks. But we did and he did. They started talking and found out they had a lot in common. A year later, they were married … and shared a common last name.

So many people got divorced during that time. My uncle got married. If he hadn't found something positive to talk about in the middle of all that chaos, they never would have found one another. And I wouldn't be sharing his story with you today.

So you never know. Don't be so quick to give up hope—in any area of your life. Don't stop trying. Don't stop believing.

We all wear masks in life. Learn to see the person behind the mask. And when you keep looking for the good … you may just find that something good is also out there looking for you.

What You Tolerate

I just ended a long-standing friendship. Done. One of my best friends. We were practically inseparable for the last four years.

But … over that time period … I allowed some boundaries to become blurred. I overlooked some major red flags. Red flags that a more careful observer would never have been able to miss.

I guess I allowed our friendship to cloud my better judgement.

And I'm not making excuses. They say that in life … you can either have excuses or results. Not both. I choose results.

And it's hard to choose results sometimes. It can be lonely. Because so many people don't. So many people in life choose to underperform, to be satisfied with mediocrity … and even worse, to be satisfied with low standards and bad behavior.

So I'm separating myself from the pack. Maybe human beings are pack animals, but we've got to fly solo sometimes. Sometimes we've got to make the decision to go it alone. I'm raising my standards … and I suggest you do the same.

Ask yourself if the people you're spending time with make you feel good about yourself when you're with them. How do you feel when you leave? Better or worse? Uplifted or downcast? Raised up or beaten down? Look for those indicators. Follow those breadcrumbs. Examine what you tolerate.

My Significant Other

I just got out of a relationship. Thought this one was my one-and-only ... my significant other. Don't ask me whose fault it was. This time ... there was enough blame to go around for both parties. Equal measures of fault. So now I'm working on myself. Trying to re-invent myself and evolve into the best version of myself I can ever possibly become.

And it's not always easy. But the goal—for all of us—is not to change who we are, but to become more like who we are when we're operating at our very best.

Intellectually, I know I'll never get to one hundred percent. Perfect is not an option. Perfection sounds good on paper, but is never rooted in reality. So the realistic goal is to evolve into the best possible version of me. And bring that new, improved version into my next relationship ... someday.

Someday ... maybe someday soon ... but not right away. Because I also need time to lick my wounds, step back, and re-evaluate. And ask myself why I haven't found my significant other yet.

Because up until now, I've always gravitated towards the wrong type of person. That's a fact. Seems like I've always dated my insignificant other.

Mike Kimmel

The Fault Lies Not in Our Stars

Do you believe in astrology? Man, oh man, I sure don't. My ex was really into it … back when we were together. Had a big, honkin' book about that stuff. It's all mumbo jumbo to me. Apparently, I'm an earth sign. My ex is a water sign. Together we made mud. I made the mistake of splashing around in that mud way too long. Nowadays, I fly solo.

George Washington said it's better to be alone than in bad company. William Shakespeare said, "the fault lies not in our stars, but in ourselves." And it's double … double, double, toil and trouble … when our selves get too deep into astrology and all that mess.

Because we shouldn't let the sun and the moon and the stars tell us who we are and what we should do. It should always be vice versa. We should tell them. After all, we named them. We gave them the names we call them by. Our scientists discovered them with our telescopes that we built. Right here on Planet Earth. Or Planet Midgard … whatever you want to call our planet.

That means we decide for the planets, stars, sun, and moon. The planets don't decide for us. It's just like my little niece says, "You're not the boss of me."

I agree with her. I agree with William Shakespeare, George Washington, and my little niece. The fault lies not in our stars … but in ourselves. See? We all agree. It's up to us. Our life is our responsibility. Take responsibility for your own actions … and inactions. Don't blame the planets.

Start Where You Stand

There's an old saying. Start where you stand. I think that's excellent advice. Because so many people out there are waiting for things to be perfect.

I don't wanna start until I'm ready. I don't wanna start until I can get it all organized. I don't wanna start until I know I can do everything right. I don't wanna start until I'm able to give it one hundred percent. I don't wanna start until I know everything's gonna turn out perfect … according to plan.

Know what it sounds like? Sounds like they don't wanna start!

But we have to start. Mary Shelley said the beginning is always today. And today's a great day to begin. We have to start putting our great ideas into action so they can become tangible. Otherwise, they remain inside your head … just a bunch of little electrical impulses bopping around from one synapse to the next inside your beautiful, bountiful brain.

Get those ideas out instead. Get them out there in the world. Put 'em on paper as a first step. Let them see the light of day. Birth them … so they'll have a birthday. Something to celebrate. They don't have to be perfect … but they can still turn out to be something worth celebrating.

Who knows? Maybe they'll turn out better than you think. Maybe they'll be excellent. But we'll never know until we make a decision and give it a starting point. Start right now. Not when it's perfect. Not next month, next week, or even tomorrow. Start now. Start where you stand.

Mike Kimmel

Choose Pineapple Juice

I'm not too good in the kitchen … but I started juicing. Do you juice? It's messy, but the results are spectacular.

Orange is my favorite. Nothing fancy. Basic nuts and bolts. Did you ever take an orange, cut it in half and squeeze? If you cut an orange in half and squeeze it, what will come out? What comes out when you squeeze an orange?

Don't over-think. It's not a trick question.

Correct. Not apple juice, not pineapple juice, not grapefruit juice. You always get orange juice. One hundred percent of the time. That's a cold-pressed fact.

Question Number Two: Why?

Because that's what's hidden inside. That's what's trapped beneath the surface … invisible to the eye. Orange juice lives within every orange. Always.

How does this affect us? Well, let's extrapolate this example to its real-life application. If somebody squeezes you … and puts pressure on you … what will come out? Does anger comes out? If jealousy, frustration, bitterness, brokenhearted-ness, and rage come out of you … then it's because that's what's inside.

Those things come out because they're hidden inside.

You might say it's because of what someone else did, how they treated you, disrespected you, and took you for granted. It's because of what *those* people did.

But usually, it's not the external thing that's the problem. It's our reaction to it. So let's agree to flip the script. Because we can't control what shows up in life to pressure us. We can't control the environment … so we must control our response to the environment.

So the next time someone pressures you, let's not give in to the temptation to respond in kind. Instead, let's just be kind … no matter what the outside world does. Let's make pineapple juice come out of that orange. Decide beforehand on the response you choose. Decide on a response that's most closely in line with the life you want to create for yourself.

Don't respond with anger. Don't take the bait. Don't treat people as bad as they are. Treat them as good as you are.

Albert and Marilyn

What's the last thing any person needs? Give up? The last thing anyone needs is more of what they already have. And that's gonna be different for everyone.

Example. A rich person doesn't really need more money. Sure, they might want it, but they probably don't really need it. A world-class athlete doesn't really need more exercise. Sure, it would be nice, but it's not really gonna change their fitness level. A collector with a million comic books or baseball cards doesn't really need one more. Right or wrong?

Nobody needs more of what they have. I think that applies in the dating world too. People look for qualities in a significant other that they may not have themselves … or that people may not see in them. That's why they say opposites attract. Makes sense, right?

Example. Back in the day, Marilyn Monroe dated Albert Einstein. They were opposites. Marilyn was famous for her looks … but she loved smart men. She was actually super-smart herself, but people didn't think of her that way because she was so beautiful. But she was always reading. Always had her nose in a book. Kinda like a scientist.

And Einstein was known for his intelligence, but he actually had a really playful side too. There's a famous picture of him riding his bicycle and sticking his tongue out at the photographer. Just being silly. And Einstein loved being in the spotlight. Kinda like an actor.

The Glamour Girl and the Brilliant Scientist. What did Albert and Marilyn talk about on their dates? Who knows? I don't have the answer. I didn't wait on their table. I wasn't a fly on that wall.

But maybe they had a lot in common. Don't be so quick to judge people by what they look like … or what society tells you to see. And let's not judge ourselves by what we look like, either … or what we do for a living. Don't ever disqualify yourself. Because Albert and Marilyn had a lot more going on underneath the surface than just "what meets the eye." All of us do. There's much more going on from the inside looking out … than other people can see from the outside looking in.

Time and Money

Have you ever noticed this unusual phenomenon? There appears to be a strange disconnect between our time and our money. Seems like we always have an overabundance of one and a corresponding shortage of the other.

I'm either making plenty of jingles and am stressed beyond belief running from one appointment or obligation to the next with no time to enjoy any of it.

Or … bored out of my flippin' mind … with all the time in the world on my hands … but nothing in my pocket except a hole … and even that's tied up with a piece of string.

I've had times when I made so much money … I'm not bragging … but I really had to restrain myself … and remind myself not to be irresponsible with it.

And there were other chapters of my life when I was unemployed for long, long stretches at a time. I was so broke I could walk by a bank and trip the alarm.

But imagine you're opening your wallet. A stranger walks by and starts pulling bills out of your wallet one by one by one. You'd probably get pretty upset with that person. I know I would. All of us would.

But think about it. People do far more damage to us every day when they make inroads upon our most valuable resource and commodity of all … our time.

We should be hyper-aware and protective of our time. We should be more concerned about people stealing our time than our money.

Because you can always make more money. You can never make more time.

Changing, Evolving, and Redirecting

Sometimes a door closes for you when you think it should open. When everybody told you it would stay open forever. Life is that way. We try things and they don't always work out the way we'd like them to.

Still … we gotta keep dreaming and believing. Never give up on your dream just because of the time it will take you to accomplish it. That time will pass anyway … whether we use it wisely or not. The time spent seeking after what we want changes us. That time and effort knocks off all our rough edges.

But in order to accomplish something we've never done before, we have to become somebody we've never been before. You have to evolve into a new kind of person on this Earth. The kind of person who can do what your heart directs you to do.

That's rare in this world. Most people are outer-directed, rather than inner-directed. They're motivated by pain. Motivated by the potential negative consequences of their actions and inactions.

Most people don't change when they see the light. Most people change when they feel the heat. Everyone starts caring when it's too late. People go through serious challenges and it changes them, I promise you. I've been around a while and I've seen it a thousand times. I've never met a strong person with an easy past.

So don't be afraid of changing and evolving. Don't be afraid of growth. Be more afraid of the opposite of growth. Be more afraid of staying the same.

One Day or Day One?

One Day or Day One? You decide. Buddha said the problem is that we think we all have time. People say time is money, but time is actually a much more valuable resource than money. We can always make more money. We can never make more time.

That's why the worst thing you can ever do for yourself is to procrastinate … to put off doing something you absolutely know you want to do with your life. Because there's always an opportunity cost … a cost we all pay for every letter or email we didn't write … every phone call we didn't make … and every action we didn't take.

So don't stop to chill. Or at least … don't stop to chill too long. If you're gonna chill, then chill in the refrigerator, not the freezer. You can rest from time to time. But don't cool your heels longer than you have to. Because we can be like ducks in the water … just chilling, just floating. We can look relaxed on the outside but, under the surface, we can still be paddling away like crazy. Going a hundred miles an hour. Maybe even a hundred miles a minute.

Because we always want to keep the end game in sight. We always want to keep the main thing the main thing. Showing people your results is much more rewarding than talking with people about your future plans. Try it. See for yourself.

Ask yourself this question. If you fix the procrastination problem in your life, what would your life look like moving forward? What would today look like for you? Will it be one day or day one?

Mike Kimmel

First Day of the Rest of Your Life

My grandfather has a funny saying. Today is the first day of the rest of your life. That's an old-fashioned expression that was popular when he was my age. But it really hits home for me today. It makes me think of something. It makes me … more introspective. I start thinking seriously about my age … now that I'm a full-fledged adult.

Grandpa made me realize that this is the oldest I've ever been … and the youngest I'm ever going to be. Most likely, anyway.

It's funny. A lot of my college friends think they're all grown up and know everything there is to know. That's not me. I'm confident … but never arrogant. Arrogance requires advertising. Confidence speaks for itself. I'm old enough to know better and young enough to understand I still have miles to go and volumes to learn.

Because at one time, I was the youngest person on the face of the Earth.

Don't laugh. You were too. No matter how old we grow, how sophisticated we become, how much we learn, and how much we earn. Remember this lesson. Guard and maintain your youthful energy, enthusiasm, and optimism. Because, once upon a time, for one brief shining moment in eternity, you were the youngest person on this planet too.

Older Than You Think

Guess what? I'm older than you might think. I'm not gonna give you the actual number … because I gotta keep some secrets. But I'm older than my parents were when they got married. I'm even older than my parents were when they were my age … or at least it feels like I am, anyway.

But I've finally gotten to the point where I stopped lying about my age … and started bragging about it.

Because time is relative. And time has no meaning except the meaning we ascribe to it. And the meaning I choose to give it has now evolved. It's evolved because I've evolved. Took me a few years, but I've arrived … if not at my perfect place, then at least to a place where I'm comfortable. Or at least relatively comfortable.

But some people are never comfortable. Not where time, the future, and their chronological age are concerned. Some people can't sit still for a minute, not even a second. They're always racing from one thing to the next. But if you're always racing to the next moment, then what happens to the one you're already living in?

So I suggest you slow things down. Savor the journey. Enjoy the ride. Take time to smell the roses … and not just hit the poses. And someday you'll wake up and find out … that you're older than you think you are too.

The Wealthiest Places

Where is the wealthiest place in the world? Can you guess?

The wealthiest places on Earth are not located in Beverly Hills, on the Miracle Mile, or Park Avenue in New York City.

Hint: the wealthiest place on Earth may be found in every big city and every small town throughout the world. The wealthiest places on our planet are … the graveyards. Because buried in those graveyards are untouched, untapped resources. Dreams that were never brought to life. Books that were never written. Movies that were never produced. Businesses that were never launched. Products that were never patented. Ideas that were never developed.

It was Horace Mann who told us that we should be ashamed to die until we have won some great victory for mankind. And Dr. Howard Thurman, who was a mentor to Dr. Martin Luther King, challenged us even more dramatically.

Dr. Thurman invited us to imagine ourselves on our deathbeds … surrounded not by our family members, but surrounded instead by the ghosts of every unborn dream, every discarded idea, and every unused talent that was given to us throughout our lifetime. And those ghosts of our unrealized potential are looking down upon us—not with love, not with reverence, not with sympathy—but with large angry eyes. And as our light diminishes, they scream out: "We came to you! We asked you to bring us to life … and you didn't do it! And now we must go down to the grave together!"

Don't let them go. Don't sentence your dreams to die a lonely, unfulfilled death. Don't cast them down into the darkness. Dedicate all your waking days instead to bringing your dreams forth into the light. Those dreams, goals, and aspirations were given to you for a reason. They were given to you to help you create your destiny.

Only you can bring them to life. Only you can rescue them from the wealthiest places on Earth.

Mike Kimmel

Time Has No Meaning

You should see my younger brother. I've never seen anyone so focused and determined in my life. He's in college for art. He specializes in painting. Oil painting. He paints these beautiful portraits. They look exactly like the people who are modeling for him too. He's painted everyone in our family already.

What's really amazing, though, is when he goes downstairs to paint. Time has no meaning for him. He has an easel and a canvas set up in our basement at home. Every day, he says, "I'm going downstairs to paint for a while."

I always say, "Define 'a while.'" Because time has no meaning for my brother when he's painting. He can go downstairs and work on his canvases for five, six, seven hours at a time. Somebody always has to go down there and knock. Somebody has to remind him to eat. Remind him to go to sleep.

I think that means this is what he's supposed to be doing with his life. Because time has no meaning when he goes into his painting vortex. Time stands still for my brother and he's not interested in anything that may distract him from his mission and purpose.

I know, people ask what can someone do with a college degree in art? I'm not exactly sure, but I know he's going to contribute a little more beauty to this world than we already have … one canvas at a time.

And maybe by his example … he can show the rest of us how to make time stand still for us too.

People May Laugh at You

A lot of people are afraid to be themselves. I mean the real you. The real them. Because a person has to do a lot of thinking to figure out who they are deep down inside, what they really want, what makes them tick, and what they really want to do with their lives. What they want from the world … and what they will agree to offer the world in return.

You've got to give something back. When you figure out what that is, more often than not, you've found your true purpose and calling in life.

When you find your purpose and calling, you become a very unusual type of person. You become a little different from the rest of the world. And that can be lonely sometimes.

People may laugh at you. They laughed at me when I figured out who I am. People laugh when they don't understand. They don't understand a person following a different path. But everyone who accomplished anything worthwhile for themselves, their families … and the world … was following a different path and pursuing their higher calling in life. They were too dedicated, too focused … and too smart to be distracted by all the background noise around them. Including other people's laughter. Some people are too smart for the world to understand.

So if people laugh at you, consider it a compliment. They laughed at a lot of other people who were too smart for the world too.

Mike Kimmel

A Transactional Process

My friend Billy is a true gentleman. Seems like it anyway. He always says "please and thank you." "Sir and "ma'am."

Best of all, he holds the door open for females. Males too, as a matter of fact. Even when they're total strangers. The other day at work, Billy held the door for seven people in a row. Seven. I was impressed. But you know how many of those seven people thanked him? Correct. Zero.

I felt kinda bad for him. Then I noticed his reaction. He felt even worse! He was shaking his head, rolling his eyes … even cursing under his breath! Definitely not acting like a true gentleman.

I told my family about it over dinner this weekend. They all know Billy. My sister asked if holding the door open was intended to be a transactional process. I didn't quite get that. So she asked if Billy was seeking a pre-determined end result in payment for his good deed of holding a door.

I still wasn't sure what she meant. So she asked if Billy holds a door open to receive a verbal "thank you" … or does Billy hold a door open out of the goodness of his heart? Good question.

Only Billy can answer that one. But it's a good question for you and I to ask ourselves. Are our good deeds in life … transactional? Do you and I perform them for pre-determined end results … or out of the genuine goodness of our hearts?

And only you and I can answer that question for ourselves. So don't be afraid to look a little closer and dig a little deeper next time you extend yourself on someone else's behalf. Don't be afraid to ask yourself the tough questions. Am I doing this out of the goodness of my heart … or in expectation of a pre-determined end result? Am I doing this in expectation of a predictable outcome in a transactional process?

Mike Kimmel

The Difference We Can't See

I went to a musical recital the other day. Classical guitar. Much different than the way they play guitar in my brother's rock and roll band. Not exactly my thing, but I had two friends in the recital. I like to be supportive when I can.

Glad I went to see 'em too, because it was truly an eye-opening experience. One of my friends was the standout in the entire program. This friend had a couple of big solos … and just absolutely knocked it out of the park. Wowed the entire audience. Very powerful performance. I was so proud to be there and see it.

My other friend … well, my other friend was okay. Played pretty well. But not nearly on the same level. Not even close.

Now here's the interesting thing … they both started classical guitar training at the same time. Started together in a college music course they took for a distribution requirement. Actually, I remember going shopping with them to buy their first guitars. But one, obviously, spends a lot more time practicing with that guitar than the other.

And there's a difference in their outer results … the difference we can see … because of the difference happening behind closed doors … the difference we can't see.

The difference we can't see is what happens when nobody's watching. I call that the invisible difference … the private time. The private time set aside for practice. The amount of time spent and the intensity of that practice are the key components of my two friends' long-term results. They determine the difference we'll all see when that private time practice makes its public debut.

It's just like anything else. We can over-perform or we can under-perform. We can practice or we can not practice. And we can fool some of the people all of the time, and all of the people some of the time. But … when it's showtime, ladies and gentlemen … I promise you, nobody can fool the audience.

Early Riser

I'm an early riser. I love getting up early. Even on my days off, believe it or not. Weekends and holidays too. If I were living out on a farm, I'd be the one waking up the roosters every morning. Yes, indeed. Four AM is my best friend. Rain, shine, sun, wind, snow, or hail. Up and at 'em bright and early … each and every day without fail.

That might sound strange to you. That's okay. Because I'm not easily offended. It sounds strange to all my college friends too … and they know me a whole lot longer and better than you do.

All my old classmates say I'm missing out. Missing out on sleeping in. Missing out on R-and-R. Missing out on the restful rhythms of the Sleepy Sandman. But really, all I'm missing out on is sleeping my life away. And sleeping my dreams away.

Because we all came to this planet to accomplish something with our lives. We were sent here for a reason. We came here with goals, dreams, hopes, plans, and aspirations. My dreams are important to me. And I don't want to sleep my dreams away … and suffocate my goals under the covers. I know there's a lot of people whose destinies are connected to my own. And I'm supposed to have a positive impact on these people. For all our sakes. For all our inter-connected destinies.

So I'm up early every day. Working, thinking, planning, analyzing, strategizing. You'd be amazed at how much you can get done when you get up a little earlier. You'd be amazed at how fast your Internet runs at four AM. How fast your mind works when you let it do its thing uninterrupted by clutter, chaos, and distractions.

But this way of living and working through life may not be for everyone. You may have an entirely different approach. That's okay. Like I said, I'm not easily offended. You don't have to do things my way. I don't have to do things your way. We can agree to disagree.

Just remember me when you need an early morning wake-up call. Everybody needs a wake-up call now and then. Call me when it's your turn. I'll be ready to assist. I'll be there for you at four AM.

Accept and Except

I'm pretty happy at my job. More or less, anyway. Been there four years with no incidents. There's things I don't like, of course, but I think that would be the case in any position. I'm relatively happy overall.

However, I was recently asked to accept a new situation … accept a new policy that's gone into effect at my job.

Most people said yes very quickly. I may end up saying yes, as well. But not just yet. This one is big … and will require a little more thought. A little more analysis and introspection. A little more than just "Yes, sir" and "Yes, ma'am."

And while I'm making up my mind … they've been pressuring me. Calling me into the office every few days. Asking if I'm going to accept all the new regulations they're creating and putting into place.

But I won't be rushed. And while I'm deciding, I'll continue to ask myself, "Will I accept?" Right now, I'm leaning towards "No."

No, I do not accept … *except* for this one time. No exceptions. Because you can't have "a little bit" of integrity in your life. My integrity is not for sale and not for rent. Integrity is an all-or-nothing proposition, something you can't put a price tag on until after you realize you've lost it. And when your integrity and peace of mind are gone, all the money you've made will never be enough to buy it back for you.

And I cannot and will not accept anything *except* the very, very best. I don't want to maintain all of my integrity, stand up for all of my principles … *except* for just this one time. I hope to keep all my character, principles, and integrity intact … no matter what they ask me, tell me, or pressure me to do at my job.

I'm still young. More or less. I'll have lots of jobs throughout my lifetime. I'll keep some jobs. I'll lose some jobs … and I'll survive, bounce back, and move on. But where do I go to get my character and integrity back after I've lost them? After I've sold them to the highest bidder?

Mike Kimmel

The Part That's Not Good

I might be a little rigid in my thinking. I'm a creature of habit. I don't know why I do the things I do, but I seem to keep doing them. Every day, every week, every month, and every year.

Example: I saw an old friend for breakfast today. At one of my favorite diners. Best omelettes, waffles, pancakes, and French Toast ever. That's a good thing.

But … unfortunately, I can't say the same for the service. I usually have to wait … quite a while. Longer than normal. Half the time the waitress ignores me. That's pretty much the pattern … with every server who's ever waited on my table at this otherwise awesome diner.

I wanted to say something, to complain. But I don't like to take the coward's way out. I didn't want to just post a negative review online. Because I didn't show up in this world to be anonymous. That's not me.

So I finally decided to talk to the manager. Got it all off my chest. "I love the food. I love the decor. Location is very convenient for me. But I definitely don't come here for the service. No … and I've been coming here for years. And over those years, I've decided that the food is good enough to put up with the less than stellar service. The *far* less than stellar service."

That's my opinion and I'm sticking to it. I know me. I'm a creature of habit. And I'm a foodie. The food is the most important element of the entire experience at any restaurant … for me,

Monologues for Young Adults

anyway. But what do most people focus on? The part of the overall experience that's not good.

Listen, I get it. People have to know their priorities. I know mine. And I know what's good about this place. My advice to you is the same advice I give myself each day. "Never let the part that's not good keep you from enjoying the part that's truly excellent."

Mike Kimmel

The Way Back

I'm trying to find my way back. Because I've been wandering a long time.

How do you find your way back home after you've been gone so long? There are no easy answers, but I'm looking for the road map. Maybe a GPS so I can accelerate the process.

I think this is called growth. Evolution. Self-discovery. Whatever. Maybe I'm just re-inventing myself. Because I was a little stuck, to tell you the truth. Stuck for way too long. I only did things, went places, and had experiences that were well within my comfort zone.

I never stretched that comfort zone. A ship in the harbor is safe, but that's not what ships are built for. I was in that rut for a long, long time. And you know what they say: the only difference between a rut and a grave is the length.

Now I'm learning to stretch. This is something I had to teach myself. Because I really like all the things I like, but now I'm also learning to appreciate all the things I don't like. That might not make sense to you, and it doesn't always make sense to me either. But I think that's the feeling we get when venturing outside of our comfort zones.

Keep your eyes on the big picture. That's my best advice for anyone who wants to travel this path. Remember why you came this way. Remember how far you've come. Remember how much you had to sacrifice.

And always remember how to find your way back home to you.

The More You Know

I'm finishing up the final essay for my Master's Degree thesis. It's been a long process … and it's the next step in my academic journey before starting work on my Ph.D.

Translation: I've been in nerd mode for over a year now.

Well … the other day, I was in the waiting room for my doctor's appointment … just a routine check-up … and they were way behind. So I was waiting and waiting and waiting.

The young lady at the front desk apologized profusely. She didn't need to. I was being a busy little bee, as my grandmother used to say … deep in nerd mode.

I was prepared with my secret weapon. Index cards. If you followed me around … and watched me for the past year … before falling asleep from boredom … you would likely never find me without a few index cards stashed away in a pocket.

I'm not boasting, but I sometimes amaze myself at how much of my Master's Degree thesis I've written this way … on index cards … and post-it notes … and the backs of envelopes … in random spare moments during the day. It's amazing how much a person can get done with something so simple. A pack of index cards from the dollar store sure goes a long way for this soon-to-be-Ph.D. candidate.

And I can't say I hatched this brilliant concept inside my own highly educated head. I got the idea from my grandmother … my beautiful, dear, departed grandmother with her fourth grade education. My grandmother, who always reminded me: "The more you know, the less you need."

Your Gifts and Talents

Sorry I'm late. I couldn't find my car. I washed it yesterday and now it's a different color than I remember. And I guess I'm … just kind of that way. Always have been … as long as I can remember.

Pretty good with all the big picture things. Going back to school. Moving cross country. Starting a new job. But it's those little things … the pesky little minutiae of human existence … that have always been … somewhat problematic for me. Maybe you can relate.

I'm not that well-organized … but I have other gifts. Creative gifts. Photography, painting, drawing, music, cooking, writing. And I've learned to focus on what I do well. My creative gifts and talents. I don't worry about … washing my car, cleaning my apartment … and organizing my sock drawer. All the pesky little minutiae of human existence.

And that's the best advice I can give anyone … including myself. Concentrate on your major gifts and talents … whatever they are … and don't beat up on yourself over the things you don't do well.

Believe me, there's a past version of you that is absolutely in awe of all your gifts and talents. That past version of you is so proud of you for everything you've done … for how far you've come. And for all you will do in the future … if you promise yourself to stay the course and stay on track.

And if you focus on developing yourself in your highest areas of accomplishment … nobody's going to care how well you clean your apartment, wash your car, or organize your sock drawer. Those things will be totally irrelevant … all the pesky little minutiae of human existence.

Mike Kimmel

The Low-Hanging Fruit

The busboy in my favorite restaurant was complaining today. Complaining about six cents. Six cents someone left on the table. He said it was a lousy tip, an insult. He couldn't give it to the waiter. So he threw it out into the street for the homeless people to find.

I told him he was wrong. People never like to hear that, though … even when they *are* wrong. I said, "Maybe it wasn't meant to be a tip. Maybe some careless customer was cleaning out their pockets and didn't want the extra two jingles slowing them down. Maybe someone dropped it."

Honestly, though, if I found those six cents on my table when I sat down to eat, you know how much I would complain? Zero, that's how much I would complain.

I don't complain. I never complain. And I'm never proud when it comes to money. There have been plenty of times in my life when I had to search through the cushions of the couch to put enough change together to buy dinner. There have also been plenty of times when I didn't own a couch. Hence, no cushions. Hence, no dinner.

So you won't find me complaining about things I interpret one way … but may have a different explanation altogether in the real world. Most people won't take the time to do that. Most people don't think that way. Most people go for the obvious … and then go for the jugular.

Most people go for the easiest explanation. They go for the obvious choice. They go for that low-hanging fruit every time. I get it. That's the easy way out and the most accessible route. I'm just saying … it wouldn't be a bad idea for all of us to start aiming higher.

Hopes, Dreams, and Aspirations

Do you have a dream for your life? It's great to dream big. Just be careful who you share your plans and dreams with. Beware of the nay-sayers.

Peter Ustinov was a wonderful old-time actor … Academy Award winner, in fact, for the movie Dr. Zhivago. Peter Ustinov said that if the world were to someday blow itself up, the last thing we would all hear would be the voice of some critic telling us that such a tragedy is not possible … it simply can't be done.

That's human nature, I think. Nay-sayer nature. Einstein talked about it too. He warned us to stay away from negative people. Einstein said negative people have the unique ability to create a problem for every solution.

So be careful who you share your dreams, goals, plans, and aspirations with. Be wary of who you take into your confidence. Don't let people talk you out of your dreams and into their reality. Because their reality is not your reality. Their limits do not have to become your limits. Their self-imposed restrictions have no power over you.

People will always try to talk you out of it when you're trying to do something important with your life. It was Samuel Glover who said:

> "Beware of those who stand aloof
> And greet each venture with reproof.
> The world would stop if it were run
> By those who say it can't be done."

That's a lot of wisdom to absorb. Samuel Glover was warning us that people will try to talk us out of doing things we know we need to do when we set big goals for ourselves. The funny thing is, though … once you get yourself in motion, start moving forward, and making some real progress towards your goals … people tend to keep quiet and get out of your way.

Samuel Glover, Peter Ustinov, and Albert Einstein. Those three were really trying to help us on our journey … wherever that journey may lead us. Because in every situation, life is asking us a question … and our actions are always the answer. Are you going to give up, give in, or give it your all? Our job is simply to answer well. Don't listen to the nay-sayers. Don't let other people stop you. Keep moving forward towards your destiny.

The Way of the World

Something just doesn't sit right with me. Something's just not adding up lately down here on Planet Earth.

People not acting right to one another any more. Businesses not showing any loyalty to their customers … or their employees. Politicians, judges, and bureaucrats forgetting the public that elevated them into those high positions in the first place. Forgetting that they were put in office to serve the public … and not the other way around.

People tell me this is the way of the world. Dog eat dog. Get the other guy before he gets you.

The way of the world. The way it's always been. Do unto others before they do unto you. Steal office supplies every chance you get. Skim a little off the top. Do your personal business during working hours. Work your side hustle while you're on the clock. Stick it to the man.

Yep. That seems to be the dominant philosophy in so many circles. Stick it to the man. He deserves it and would definitely do the same to you if the roles were reversed. That's the way of the world.

But maybe it doesn't have to be that way any more. Maybe there are other options for the way we treat each other … and the way business is conducted … down here on Planet Earth. Just because that's the way things are …. doesn't mean that things have to be the way they've always been.

Because this world is round, my friends. What goes around comes around. This world turns on an axis. We can turn it in a different direction instead. I'm not saying it will be easy, but I am saying it will be worth it.

And maybe, just maybe, we can change the way things spin. Maybe every one of us can change that spin, change that direction, and begin to change the way of the world.

Big Plans

I just moved into a new place. My first time in my very own place ... that I have all to myself. Biggest space I've ever lived in too. Just me.

No roommates. No couch surfers. No significant others. No insignificant others. Just me. Got that? Just me.

I think I really lucked out this time around. You know what they say. Fortune favors the bold. Guess I finally started thinking bigger. Like my Uncle Matt always told me to do.

But a lot of people ... kinda don't get that. Like this guy who came in to fix the window right after I moved in. One of the windows wasn't closing properly. Which is fine. There's always a couple things that need our attention.

But this window guy copped a little bit of an attitude with me. He gave me a look. You know what I mean by "a look?" Yeah. One of those. Then he asked, "Why did you move into such a big place?" And he had this little smirk on his face too ... which I really didn't care for.

I told him, "Why did I move into such a big place? Because I've got big plans." That shut him up right away. Then he went back to work fixing the window... which is why he was there in the first place.

But this was a wake up call for me. Just because you start thinking bigger doesn't mean the rest of the world is going to show up and be on board too. You can't bring everyone with you on your journey. And you're not supposed to. Because thinking bigger is outside a lot of people's comfort zones. We can't force them to see the world the way we see it. All we can do is become our best selves and set a good example. That gives them the opportunity to catch up or shrink back.

Personally, I'm done shrinking. No more shrinking—internally or externally. I'm expanding. From now on, I'm all about expansion. Because my comfort zone has grown exponentially. It now completely fills this entire, gigantic space I am privileged to call my new home.

Mike Kimmel

The Steroid Question

I come from a family of athletes. More or less. Some better than others, of course, but all athletes just the same. All my brothers and sisters won letters in varsity sports all through high school and college. A couple of them went even further when they could and played pro and semi-pro sports after graduation. Tried to stay committed to their athletic competitions of choice for the long haul … even after receiving those college degrees. That's not easy to do, so I give 'em credit. It's much easier to just settle in with a regular job-job and relegate yourself to weekend warrior status for life … just like all your old teammates.

As for me, I got hooked for a few years post-graduation on the heavy weights. Powerlifting and even a little Olympic style lifting for flexibility. Once you start attacking that heavy iron, it's like you're playing a game of chicken. Seeing how heavy you can go before an injury stops you for good. And if you manage to stay injury free, you eventually come face to face with the Deadly Dilemma of the Barbell Game. The steroid question. To juice or not to juice. Take that poison or step away from it.

I had just arrived at that decision point … and I chose to step away from it.

Because all athletes eventually reach the limits of their natural potential … physically, at least. Mentally is another story. But you can go only so far—and no further—physically. Steroids push athletes past those natural limits … for those willing to roll the dice and deal with the potential consequences.

In the Iron Game, the top three finishers at every major meet were all juice-monsters. Sure, you could keep entering those contests and finish no higher than fourth place. No trophies for fourth and below. No trophies, but also no deadly steroid consequences. I can live with that.

And, … you know what? I can buy myself a trophy. A big, giant, first place trophy. First place for making good, sound, healthy decisions. First place for thinking long-term. First place for protecting my health. First place for saving my own life.

Mike Kimmel

Change Your Hat

Are you like me? Have you missed the mark a time or two? Have you secretly wished that you had stepped up and done better … because you knew deep down in your heart that you could do better?

I think we've all been there. But instead of beating up on ourselves, ask this question. What is the greatest ideal of myself I can be today? Today. Not tomorrow. Not next week, next year, or when everybody starts appreciating and respecting you. Not when all your life circumstances line up properly.

Today. Just for today, how can I be the very best me?

This is the way. This is how you do it. This is how you make small, significant changes in your life. Ready?

Change your hat. That's right. Your hat. Because we all wear different hats in life.

We wear the pleasant hat with strangers, the friendly hat with casual acquaintances, the warm, nurturing hat with our spouses or significant others, the protective, mentoring hat with our children, the analytical collaborator hat with our co-workers, and the deadly weapon hat with people we need to keep at a safe distance.

But when things start going sideways in life, it's a good idea to change hats. When a problem comes up that makes your emotions run wild, address it with your analytical hat. When there's a conflict at work, put on your statesman hat. When there's a problem at home, put on your mentorship hat.

Which hat will you wear today? Will you be at your best today … or will you allow your emotions to bounce you around like a helpless rag doll? With which version of yourself do you most closely identify today? Which version of you would be best suited to deal with the problem at hand?

Don't be afraid to ask yourself the hard questions. And when you feel things going the wrong way in life, don't be afraid to change hats.

Mike Kimmel

A New Old Friend

My uncle did something amazing. He contacted this lady … a lady from his past.

Uncle Jack … for years … said he was absolutely "ga-ga" over this woman … but their timing was terrible. He was going through a rough time. She was going through a rough time. And it's hard for people to connect like they could when they're both facing challenges on their own.

Okay. So now he contacts her. Out of the blue. After not speaking a word to one other for fourteen years. A long, long time.

They never exactly … dated. They weren't boyfriend and girlfriend. But they spent a lot of time together. They were very close … just not … in that way.

He found her again on social media. They got together for coffee a couple of weeks ago. Very cordial. He told this woman he always liked her, always appreciated her friendship … and thought about her often through the years.

And she told him … just about the same thing. Okay. So now they had their coffee. Just like when they used to get coffee at their favorite old spot years ago. Then they met a second time for coffee. Great. Then they had a nice lunch together at a very fancy restaurant.

You don't know my uncle, but he never goes to fancy restaurants. So I knew things were looking good. And I ask Uncle Jack how everything's going.

He says … no expectations. Sometimes you just want someone in your life to talk to … who knows you, appreciates you, and accepts you as you are. Sometimes you need a new friend. And if it's a new old friend … then you've even got some history together. That's even better. But still … no pressure. No judgment. No expectations.

Okay, Uncle Jack. No expectations. Fine. Have it your way. Take things nice and slow with this woman from your past, this woman of your dreams. But you know what I'm thinking? Maybe … just maybe … after fourteen years … maybe your timing's not so terrible anymore.

Time Wounds All Heels

I'm newly single. Single again, I should say. Surprise, surprise.

Thought I'd be … double by now. I thought this was it. Thought this person was the one. Thought this latest romantic entanglement would lead me down the aisle … instead of down the primrose path.

No excuses. Everybody warned me. Warned me to take it slow. Warned me to keep my eyes and ears open and my wits about me. Everybody told me. Family, friends… and even people I thought didn't like me very much … they warned me to keep away from my soon-to-be ex.

Guess they saw something I didn't. Guess I had to find out a few things for myself … and learn this lesson the hard way. Guess I finally did.

But it's one thing to split with someone … and another thing entirely for that person to slander your name, badmouth you all over town, and go out of their way to make trouble for you at your job. And then sabotage your personal finances by draining your bank account and running up your credit card. Totally against the rules. Like having a mortal enemy living inside your own camp.

Moving forward, I've slowly begun to see the light. Started to recognize all the red flags I never saw before. Funny thing is … do you know how much I want to get back at this person? How much I secretly long for revenge? How much I want people to hear my side? How much I want to clear my name? How much I want to be vindicated?

Zero, zero, zero, zero, and zero.

But I do need time to step away and be by myself. That's all I'm asking right now. Because I know intuitively that time will soften this blow.

And I am not even remotely interested in extracting revenge on anyone who hurt me in the past. In fact, I wish them all the best. I hope they can find peace. But karma has a funny way of coming back around … because this world is round.

They say time heals all wounds. I believe that. And I've also seen that … time wounds all heels.

Mike Kimmel

The Nicest Man I Ever Knew

We buried my Uncle Bill last month. My favorite uncle. The nicest man I ever knew. Uncle Bill would do anything for you. Never turned down an honest request. Heart of gold. Always put other people first. That was my Uncle Bill.

Little bit of a packrat, though, and he accumulated all kinds of stuff over his lifetime … stashed it away in cardboard boxes, plastic bins, and old grocery bags … along with all his notebooks, diaries, and journals. Magazines and newsletters he sent away for … letters he sent and received. Correspondences he maintained with people we never met. Always scribbling away in his little notebooks. He carried them everywhere. That was my Uncle Bill … always writing stuff down.

I've been helping Aunt Betty go through it all. Can't believe what we found. Drawings, diagrams, notes about all the things he was planning. Ideas for products, inventions, and stories. Things that really looked good on paper … some very strong ideas. We found booklets and applications for copyrights, trademarks, and patents … that Uncle Bill never filled out. Never mailed in. All the books, articles, short stories, and blog posts he was writing. All the inventions he planned to register … someday.

We found recipes, logos, slogans, and diagrams … all kinds of wonderful ideas for a restaurant chain … a fast-food franchise Uncle Bill never talked about … and never got around to launching. No feasibility study. No test marketing. No stock offering. No IPO.

I'm learning a lot about my uncle, his hidden plans, and his secret life. The life he never shared … and never finished. We never knew my uncle was so smart … and so scared. Yes, scared. He must have been scared to have all these wonderful plans and ideas … and never act on any of them.

I don't believe Uncle Bill died all at once. I believe he died a little bit at a time each day.

Because every time you hold something back, you die a little bit inside. Every action you don't take … takes something from you. Every unspoken word, every unsent letter or email, every unkept promise robs you of a little piece of your destiny. It whittles you down, one millimeter at a time, until finally there's nothing left … except the hollow shell that once held your spirit, your future, and your unique, personal calling on this Earth.

I miss my Uncle Bill. I miss him like crazy. He was my favorite uncle and I loved him dearly. The nicest man I ever knew. And the smartest man I never knew.

Mike Kimmel

He Was Gorgeous

I want to tell you about a very unusual person in American cultural history. They called him the Human Orchid, Gorgeous George. Maybe you've heard of him.

Gorgeous George was an old time pro wrestler, the most famous wrestler of the 1950s and a consummate showman. Say what you will about wrestling, but this guy was one of the top performers … and a marketing genius. They said that Gorgeous George and Milton Berle sold more television sets than anyone else back in the early, pioneering days of black and white TV.

Gorgeous George played a specific character on TV … the bleached blond bad guy. Pro wrestling has good guys and bad guys. Cowboys in white hats and cowboys in black hats. It's a proven formula for success in that industry. And Gorgeous George always gave it 100 percent. Never out of character. That guy was all in.

He played his character 24-7 … in and out of the ring. Had his name legally changed from George Wagner to Gorgeous George. Had a valet accompany him to the ring dressed in a tuxedo and carrying a fancy atomizer filled with perfume on a silver tray. Gorgeous George wouldn't get in the ring until his valet sprayed the ring, his opponent, and the referee's hands with perfume.

One time, he had to talk with a wrestling promoter after the show. Everybody had already left the arena but Gorgeous wouldn't set foot into that man's office until his valet sprayed the entire room with perfume. You understand why? Even though nobody else was around, Gorgeous knew that the promoter would tell that story hundreds of times through the years. Fantastic word-of-mouth publicity.

Another time, they brought him to Australia. Thousands of people showed up at the airport. Packed the runway. Gorgeous started thinking, "What do I do? What's my angle? How can I use this?"

He let all the other passengers disembark. And he made all those people wait. He refused to get off the plane until they brought him the most beautiful woman in Australia … to accompany him down that long flight of stairs.

Like I said, he was all in … way back before we had the Internet, cell phones, and social media to promote ourselves. So whenever you and I are tempted to do things half way … let's remember our old friend Gorgeous George. Gorgeous would encourage all of us to step out of our comfort zones. When we do, we'll never want to go back again. Start today. This world needs every one of us at our gorgeous best. Stop holding back. We all need to be the 100-percenters we were meant to be in life.

Mike Kimmel

Post-Pandemic Pleasures

Ah, what a thrill. What a glorious day it is! I am so happy today. Smiling so wide I can eat a banana sideways.

Never thought I'd look forward to … the basic human contact of going to the bank and waiting on line. Hate to say it, but this has become the highlight of my week nowadays.

And it's not just the bank, believe me. I have the time of my life going to the post office, the dry cleaners, and getting the oil changed in my car.

And don't even ask me about getting my tires rotated. That's like Christmas morning. Those guys at the tire shop have complimentary coffee and donuts in the customer waiting area. That might be the highlight of … maybe my whole year. Though they recommend rotating your tires quarterly, which is fine with me.

It's funny how you can learn to appreciate the simple things in life … after they've been taken away from you for two years.

These are the things my grandfather called the simple, mundane tasks we've all got to deal with on a daily basis. But I call them my Post-Pandemic Pleasures.

And pleasures they surely are. It doesn't take much to make me happy, as you can plainly see. A lot less than it used to … pre-pandemic, that is. And that's what I wish for you too … and for all of us that were shut down, locked in, and isolated for so long. That we can learn to appreciate the simple little everyday tasks in life. That we can learn to appreciate our Post-Pandemic Pleasures.

"We would never learn to be brave and patient if there were only joy in the world."

~ Helen Keller

"There will come a time when you believe everything is finished. That will be the beginning."

~ Louis L'Amour

Afterword: Two Suggestions on Performance

Please feel free to adapt these monologues to fit your own unique background, ethnicity, age, point of view, physical type, and skill set. If you find it helpful to make a minor change in a character's name, background, occupation, locale, or other script detail when crafting your own performances from this book—then please feel free to do so.

These were never meant to be "cookie cutter" scripts. One size definitely does not fit all. I often tell my acting students, "it's my book, but it's your audition." Make a change if you feel it will help you. We're all very different, and a minor change in a script can create a powerful difference in a performance. As long as the changes are small ones—and you are able to remain true to the overall intention of the storylines—I am certain these monologues will still work well for you.

Improvisation

When I work with actors in class—or in private coaching sessions—we often apply improvisation techniques to our scenes and monologues. Improv is a wonderful discipline for actors and helps us find layers and nuances in scripts that would otherwise remain hidden. Improv is an outstanding tool to help us dig deeper into the script and go far beyond what's just written on the surface.

If you haven't trained in improv, I strongly encourage you to do so. It's a skill that will do you a world of good throughout your acting career. There's a very practical reason for this. Very often on stage and screen something will go wrong unexpectedly. Actors who are able to improvise an additional line of dialogue to cover the glitch can save the scene. Believe me, producers and directors notice (and appreciate) these skills in actors. They know that actors with solid improvisational skills can save their production time and money by helping to avoid additional takes, setups, and reshoots. If you're new to improv and need a good starting point, then try adding one or two additional lines of dialogue to the piece you've selected. This is a very effective way to begin working on a new monologue. It can also help keep your performance fresh when practicing a script you're been working on for a very long time.

The Moment Before

Another valuable question to ask yourself is: "Where was I—and what was happening in the scene—right before this monologue interrupted me?" Many acting teachers refer to this as "the moment before," but we can dig even deeper. Pretend that your monologue is part of a full-length script. Decide what was physically happening right before you allowed yourself to become interrupted. What made you stop, react—and then perform this particular monologue on this particular day for this particular audience? Can you see how much more this gives you to work with—rather than just focusing on memorizing, getting every word exactly right, and making sure all the sentences are in the right order?

Try to make any additional details you add as specific as possible. Generalities tend to bring about confusion and misinterpretation, causing actors to lose focus and direction. Specific details always open us up to increased possibilities for more creative "jumping off" points. Think of specific details you might add to the script as launchpads for improvisation. This will help you dive right into your monologue as if it was an important personal message, epiphany, or realization that has just occurred to you. It's so important, in fact, that you need to stop and share this message with your audience.

The overall objective in writing these monologues has been to build and maintain a logical, sequential flow for the storylines and a conversational, user-friendly approach to character development, inner dialogue, and pacing. Keep these ideas in mind when rehearsing and I believe you'll find that these monologues will be relatively easy to memorize, as well.

"Every man must decide whether he will walk in the light of creative altruism."

~ Martin Luther King Jr.

A Request

I hope you will have great success performing these monologues in your acting classes and auditions. If you've enjoyed ***Monologues for Young Adults***—and feel that it could benefit other actors and teachers—then please consider leaving a brief book review on the merchant site where you purchased it (or your favorite book-review website and/or online retailer).

Book reviews are extremely important for both authors and readers. They are much appreciated by both. Reviews help spread the word to readers looking for material in a specific genre, and also help authors reach a larger readership. Even one brief line or two makes a very big difference.

Additionally, please consider recommending this book to your local public library or school library. Schools and libraries can often purchase books at a significant discount. In this way, the book can be made available to readers who may not be able to purchase their own copies.

Mike Kimmel

Recommended Reading

Acting for Films and TV by Leslie Abbott

Acting in Film by Michael Caine

Acting in Television Commercials for Fun and Profit by Squire Fridell

Adventures in the Screen Trade by William Goldman

An Actor Prepares by Constantin Stanislavski

An Agent Tells All by Tony Martinez

Audition by Michael Shurtleff

The Backstage Actor's Handbook by Sherry Eaker

Being an Actor by Simon Callow

A Book by Desi Arnaz

The Courage to Create by Rollo May

Do One Thing Every Day That Scares You by Robie Rogge

The Dramatic Writer's Companion by Will Dunne

Ego is the Enemy by Ryan Holliday

Four Screenplays by Syd Field

Free Play: Improvisation in Life and Art by Stephen Nachmanovitch

The Godfather Notebook by Francis Ford Coppola

The Great Movies by Roger Ebert

Greenlights by Matthew McConaughey

The Hidden Persuaders by Vance Packard

Hollywood by Charles Bukowski

Hollywood Babylon by Kenneth Anger

How I Made a Hundred Movies in Hollywood and Never Lost a Dime by Roger Corman

How to Act and Eat at the Same Time by Tom Logan

How to Avoid the Cutting Room Floor by Jordan Goldman

How to Get Ideas by Jack Foster

How to Make it in Hollywood by Linda Buzzell

Impro by Keith Johnstone

Improvisation for the Theater by Viola Spolin

It Would Be So Nice if You Weren't Here by Charles Grodin

Know Small Parts by Laura Cayouette

The Laws of Human Nature by Robert Greene

Live Cinema by Francis Ford Coppola

Love, Lucy by Lucille Ball

Making Movies by Sidney Lumet

Making Movies Work by Jon Boorstin

Meeting of Minds by Steve Allen

Mighty Minutes by Jim Hall

Movie Speak by Tony Bill

Mike Kimmel

My Rendezvous with Life by Mary Pickford
Ogilvy on Advertising by David Ogilvy
100 Years, 100 Stories by George Burns
On Screen Acting by Edward and Jean Porter Dmytryk
A Pictorial History of the Silent Screen by Daniel Blum
The Pocket Muse by Monica Wood
The Power of Myth by Joseph Campbell
A Practical Handbook for the Actor by Melissa Bruder
Purple Cow by Seth Godin
Reading the Silver Screen by Thomas C. Foster
Sanford Meisner on Acting by Sanford Meisner
Stella Adler: The Art of Acting by Stella Adler
Tips: Ideas for Actors by Jon Jory
True Strength by Kevin Sorbo
Understanding Movies by Louis Giannetti
Who is Michael Ovitz? by Michael Ovitz
Wild Bill Wellman: Hollywood Rebel by William Wellman Jr.

Performing Arts Books by Mike Kimmel

Youngsters:

Acting Scenes for Kids and Tweens
Monologues for Kids and Tweens
Monologues for Kids and Tweens II

Teenagers:

Scenes for Teens
Monologues for Teens
Monologues for Teens II
One-Minute Monologues for Teens

College and Adult:

Monologues for Adults
Monologues for Young Adults
Six Critical Essays on Film

Mike Kimmel

About Valerie Marsch

Valerie Marsch was born and raised in a small midwest town, population of 491. She came out of the womb wanting to be a model. Her Bible was Eileen Ford's book of Modeling, ***Secrets of the Model's World***. It was adhered to her right arm. Her goal was getting into the Ford Modeling Agency, which was the largest and best in the world. In her small town, people expressed their doubts about her going to New York City to become a model. "They will eat you there," one special person said to her. Nevertheless, Valerie finished college and off she went.

Arriving in New York City, Valerie created a plan to meet Eileen Ford. She wrote up some talking points, picked up the phone in her room at the Barbizon Hotel for Women, and dialed the Ford Modeling Agency. The first receptionist told her: "Eileen Ford has over 5,000 model applicants per month. She *may* select one for an interview." On her seventeenth try, Eileen Ford answered the phone herself. Ms. Ford wanted to know why she was calling all day. Nevertheless, Valerie got an interview and was accepted into the Ford Modeling Agency!

Next, she was one of only three models selected to go to Paris for a yearlong training program through the agency. After returning to America, Valerie continued training, auditioning, and developing "her look." She went on to represent many companies and shoot hundreds of campaigns and thousands of ads, including Revlon, Lancôme, Glamour Magazine, Good Housekeeping, Modern Bride, The Wiz, many hairstyle magazines, and worked with many catalog houses. In time, she moved from fashion to commercial lifestyle projects. This led to representing IBM, Nestea, Post Cereal, ABN Amro Bank—and shooting many magazine covers, including New York Magazine, Self Magazine, and Business Week.

Valerie is a strong union advocate and member of SAG-AFTRA and AEA. Whenever she wasn't working, she was in classes for movement, voice, commercials, teleprompter, and acting. Commercials can pay residuals for many years. Actors always appreciate this since they do so much work for little or no money throughout their careers. Valerie shot over 100 commercials, including Duracell, Lysol Pine Action, The National Enquirer, Campho Phenique, Tetris (Tetris-ized), Trump's Castle, Nintendo, Progresso Soup, Preparation H, The Ground Round, Hood Lite Ice Cream, and Michelob Beer. Print ads and campaigns also have renewal options with opportunities for models to earn excellent pay. (A drawback is that actors are unable to work for competing products for the contracted period of the renewal.)

Valerie co-hosted a talk-adventure show, **On the Water**, for more than a year with Bill Tatum. It was shot on waterways throughout the U.S., Virgin Islands, and the Caribbean and aired on cable television. A favorite TV project was working on sketch comedy for **Late Night with Conan O'Brien** on NBC. In the audition, Conan asked her to make him laugh. Valerie looked him right in the eye and said, "I will show you my checkbook." She got the part and appeared on the show dozens of times until they finally relocated to California.

Mike Kimmel

About Mike Kimmel

Mike Kimmel is a former pro wrestler and circus magician. Nowadays, he is a film, television, stage, and commercial actor and acting coach. He is a twenty-plus year member of SAG-AFTRA with extensive experience in both the New York and Los Angeles markets. He has worked with directors Francis Ford Coppola, Robert Townsend, Craig Shapiro, and Christopher Cain among many others. TV credits include **Game of Silence**, **Zoo**, **Treme**, **In Plain Sight**, **Cold Case**, **Breakout Kings**, **Memphis Beat**, **Suit Up**, **Buffy The Vampire Slayer**, and **The Oprah Winfrey Show**. He was a regular sketch comedy player on **The Tonight Show**, performing live on stage and in pre-taped segments with Jay Leno for eleven years.

Mike has appeared in dozens of theatrical plays on both coasts, including Radio City Music Hall, Equity Library Theater, Stella Adler Theater, Double Image Theater, The Village Gate, and Theater at the Improv. He trained with Michael Shurtleff, William Hickey, Ralph Marrero, Gloria Maddox, Harold Sylvester, Wendy Davis, Amy Hunter, Bob Collier, and Stuart Robinson. He holds a B.A. from Brandeis University and an M.A. from California State University at Dominguez Hills.

He has taught at Upper Iowa University, University of New Orleans, University of Phoenix, Glendale Community College, Nunez Community College, Delgado Community College, and in the Los Angeles, Beverly Hills, and Burbank, California public school districts. He is a two-time past president of New Orleans Toastmasters, the public speaking organization.

Mike has written and collaborated on numerous scripts for stage and screen. **In Lincoln's Footsteps**, his full-length historical drama on Presidents Lincoln and Garfield, was a semi-finalist in the National Playwrights Conference at the Eugene O'Neill Theater Center. Mike also received the Excellence in Teaching Award from Upper Iowa University in 2014.

In 2019, the Independent Author Network selected Mike's third book, **Monologues for Teens**, as their Performing Arts Book of the Year. In 2022, Best Indie Book Award (BIBA) chose **Monologues for Adults** as their annual winner in the Performing Arts Category. Mike is also prominently featured in Francis Ford Coppola's groundbreaking book on his innovative theater-film hybrid process, **Live Cinema**.

Mike is a full voting member of the National Academy of Television Arts and Sciences, the organization that produces the Emmy Awards each year. This is his tenth book in the Performing Arts.

Made in the USA
Columbia, SC
29 October 2024

f724042e-25ac-4bbc-aa92-9fc591026cfeR01